Darkness
Before
Dawn

Darkness
Before
Dawn

Redefining the
Journey Through
Depression

An Anthology
edited by Tami Simon

SOUNDS TRUE
BOULDER, COLORADO

Sounds True
Boulder, CO 80306

This work is solely for personal growth and education. It should not be
treated as a substitute for professional assistance such as psychotherapy,
counseling, or medical advice. In the event of physical or mental distress,
please consult with appropriate health-care professionals.

Published 2015

Cover design by Karen Polaski
Book design by Beth Skelley

Printed in the United States of America

Library of Congress Cataloging-in-Publication Data
Darkness before dawn : redefining the journey through depression :
an anthology / edited by Tami Simon.
     pages cm
  Includes index.
  ISBN 978-1-62203-410-9
  1. Depression, Mental—Case studies. I. Simon, Tami, editor.
  RC537.D297 2015
  616.85'27—dc23
                                    2014035773

Ebook ISBN 978-1-62203-451-2

10 9 8 7 6 5 4 3 2 1

Contents

Contents

Introduction

Tami Simon
Founder and Publisher, Sounds True

About ten years ago, I was participating in an advanced meditation training led by Reginald A. Ray, a pioneering teacher in the lineage of Tibetan Buddhist meditation master Chögyam Trungpa Rinpoche. At the retreat, a participant stood up at the mic and shared quite movingly about her depression and the challenges she was experiencing. After some dialogue with this student, Reggie looked at all of us in the room, about seventy people, and asked, "How many of you are depressed?" About 10 percent of the participants raised their hands.

He then said, "You are the most intelligent people in the room."

This was quite a moment for me, because *I* wanted to be one of the most intelligent people in the room. But I had no idea what Reggie was talking about. Why would the people suffering from depression be considered the most intelligent people in the room? What was I missing?

A few years ago, my partner was on a trip to Africa for a month, and I had the chance to be alone in our home working on a special project. During this time, I spent an inordinate number of hours not working on anything in particular but instead lying on our upstairs couch staring into space, feeling completely blah. Everything seemed grey and meaningless; I couldn't find anything around which to orient. Why should I change my clothes or be productive or do much of anything? All the projects I was involved in tasted like ash in my mouth; everything I was up to seemed "suspicious," filled with some type of inflated ambition, some need to be someone or something in the midst of a universe that did not have a single reference point. How could I have fooled myself into investing so much heart and significance into so many activities that were essentially meaningless?

Lying on the couch in this grey fog, I flashed on Reggie's comment about the intelligence of depression and then recalled a statement I had heard attributed to Chögyam Trungpa Rinpoche: "Depression is the closest conditioned state to the awakened state."

In that moment, I had an inkling of what the intelligence of depression might be. Stripped of illusions and ambitions and the sense that anything I could come up with might ultimately matter, I actually felt . . . free. Like a balloon that had been punctured, I had fallen without any air to the earth. My experience of "utter greyness" humbled me and stopped me in my tracks. I had been stripped down. This "grey depression" helped me see the self-orientation that was motivating many of my actions, and it helped me drop this orientation and fall instead into a wide and open, boundless space.

As you will read in *Darkness Before Dawn,* there are many different types of depression, with different degrees, shades of experience, and mysterious dimensions. It is important not to lump all types of depression together—oftentimes, people use the word *depression* to refer to quite different states of being, from melancholy to situational grief to chronic despair and more. We need a nuanced approach, one that takes depression out of the purely medical category and enables us to see, each one of us in our own life, what depression is asking of us and, maybe, what it is even offering.

Personally, I don't have any experience with clinical depression or the deeply debilitating experiences that it can bring. What I do have is a desire to open up a conversation in our culture about depression, whatever its form or extent.

If you are someone who is finding themselves at this very moment in a debilitating depression, please know that you are not alone, that the team at Sounds True who created this book is reaching out to you with an outstretched hand. To support you, we have created a resource guide at the end of this book, "Resources for Suicidal Depression and Ways to Help Yourself and Others," which we hope will prove useful and beneficial to you.

Darkness Before Dawn was created with a vision of bringing openness and spiritual illumination to the journey through depression.

Throughout the process, our guiding principle has been to bring depression out of the shadows and out of a narrow medical model to instead place it rightly as part of the sacredness of the human journey. As this anthology reveals, some of the great spiritual writers and teachers of our time have journeyed through intense periods of depression and have found profound meaning in their experiences. Some have found a deep acceptance of the reality of suffering in themselves and the world; others were able to make friends with a part of their experience they had rejected. A few actually found ways to regard their depression as a signal from deep within, or even to use it as creative fuel or a point of connection with all of humanity. As you will see, the meanings drawn are diverse and individual, but they are joined by the common desire to redefine depression not simply as a disease or a pathological state but as part of the spiritual path.

In creating this anthology, I had the chance to interview several leading authors and teachers about their personal journeys through depression. It was so odd to me that during each of these interviews I experienced tremendous joy and elation. In fact, there were many days when it was totally clear to me that the highlight of that day would be spending two hours talking to someone about their darkest, most depressive experiences. How could this be? My sense is that the joy I felt came from releasing a bound-up cultural energy. Depression has been sealed off, kept underground and undiscussed. The interviews felt to me like a "coming out," a liberation of truths that can now shine brightly and light the way for others.

While editing the essays and interviews included in *Darkness Before Dawn,* I have been thinking of *you*—someone who might be suffering from depression or know someone who is that you care about. This book is designed as an open-ended exploration to help you redefine depression as an intrinsic part of the human journey. It is not meant to "fix you," but to inspire you in your own way to find the intelligence in your experience. Feel free to dip into whatever contributions inspire you and read them in whatever order you wish. *Darkness Before Dawn* is not prescriptive; it is designed to befriend you and accompany you.

Finally, I would like to offer a special moment of gratitude to Karla McLaren for the title *Darkness Before Dawn*. This is a phrase that comes from Karla's work as an empath, someone who is fluent in the language of emotions. Her work is a great gift in helping people understand the life-changing wisdom that is contained in all of our emotional experiences. Thank you, Karla, for such a fitting title for this book!

And my gratitude to all of the readers of *Darkness Before Dawn*. In a culture that primarily values what is bright and shiny and glittery, it takes great courage to descend and embrace the value in every state of being. May all of our work together help bring balance to a culture that desperately needs to learn to honor the holiness of what is dark and disowned.

1

Depression, Meditation, and the Spiritual Journey

Reginald A. Ray, PhD

The reason depression is so powerful is because you actually have to let go of pretty much everything you think or have thought in order to explore it. You have to let go of your hopes, your fears, your ambitions, the things that are working, the things that aren't working—your whole world. That's why depression is so powerful for spiritual practice: because if you step into it, it is actually a process of letting go of your entire known self.

One of the difficulties with this term *depression* is that it has such a negative connotation in contemporary society. Just using the word can be a way of discrediting what we're going through. In modern culture, depression is more or less automatically something that is undesirable. You hear it used for almost any state of mind that people find to be down and difficult. For spiritual practitioners, I think it is important to just let that label go—it's not really very useful; we need to look at "depression" freshly. We need to try to see its possibilities and potentialities, and even why it may be happening to us in the first place, as a critical and perhaps necessary step in our own journey. We need to learn to work with the energy of depression. It's fluid, and it's very, very painful, but there's really nothing to be afraid of. We need to be fully present to it, explore it, work with it, and see what happens. The pain is real and raw and undeniable, but it doesn't mean there's a problem here. If we can take the labeling and negative judgment out of it, then we can start to find out what's really going on and recognize the opportunities it is offering us.

Periodic depression, of one kind or another, is probably part of the experience of every person on the planet—where the energy of engagement with the world just isn't there, for external reasons or internal reasons, and we take a different view of our life. Suddenly, we see that a lot of the things in which we've invested so much of our energy and hope are in fact not legitimate. They're not valid; they're not real. In fact, they might not even exist, and the energy just drops into a big space of openness, emptiness, and, sometimes, overwhelming sadness. If we can't recognize the value of this periodic dismantling of our investment in the external world—if we label it a bad thing—then our response is going to be to turn against our depressive state of mind; we will then do whatever it is we do to control or simply check out of our experience. Frequently, in too forcefully encouraging us to "get better," the people around us will only drive us deeper into this avoidance—"Why can't you be connected with life? Why don't you have a positive attitude? Get over it." All of this pressure, both from others and generated internally, leaves no space for our actual experience and pushes us to cover over and deny the state we're in.

This is the challenge of living in a culture where anything on the painful side of the spectrum is regarded as being a bad thing, something that must be controlled, avoided, denied, or even destroyed, such as with heavy-duty psychotropic prescriptions. In our culture, we have so many ways to try to eliminate any state of mind we find uncomfortable—through psychiatric medications, recreational drugs, alcohol, our electronic devices, the Internet, television, consumerism, or simply keeping busy all the time. We seem to have little or no respect for our human experience, as such.

What we seem to be largely unwilling to deal with or even face is simply the way human life is given to us: the facts of life and death, of pleasure and pain, of health and disease, of success and failure, the facts of day and night, the facts of storms and sunshine. This is the human condition, and this has been the human condition going back all the way through the primates, even to the beginning of life itself; as a human being, you are going to have to experience everything. You can't just factor out one side of the equation, because then nothing happens. Life isn't easy; it shouldn't be easy. If life's easy, you're dead; there's nothing happening. Life is a challenge, and it should be a challenge. That's how people grow; it's the only way people grow.

If we read the great spiritual classics, in all the great religions, we hear that those moments of almost transcendent sadness, those moments when we suddenly see the futility of our ordinary activities, *those* are the great transition points on the journey. Those are the moments when we step back, almost as if the seeds of our external life have gone underground in winter to germinate, waiting for the moment when they can begin to grow again and appear above the ground.

Depression is a time of spiritual hibernation. If we know how to be with depression and journey through it, it is extraordinarily significant and impactful, but our belief system has enormous potential to get in the way. Whether we fall into thinking that we're going to live forever, that our "self" is real, or that depression or another challenging psychological experience is a negative thing to be denied or fixed, then the life journey, the spiritual journey—for they are one and the same—becomes very, very difficult.

Although challenging psychological experiences such as depression are part of the path and the unfolding of the meditative process, if we aren't approaching them from this perspective, it's going to be very hard for us to actually accept them and reap the benefits of doing so.

The meditator never takes anything for granted. It doesn't matter if you run into a state of mind you've experienced seemingly a million times; if you look closely, you'll see that it's actually always a new thing—and we have to find out what it is. If you can do that with a state of mind like depression, the experience will be very, very fruitful.

When we run into a very low state of mind—what we would call depression—at that point we usually check out and stop examining it: "Oh, I'm depressed." And then we start thinking about it in the way we usually do: it's some big problem, something really scary, something we have to modify or change as soon as possible, something that is getting in the way of what we want to accomplish, and so on.

But we could look at depression simply for what it is in itself: an extraordinarily powerful energy. It's an energy that is very dark, very hidden, very low; it's *nothing*, from a certain point of view, from ego's point of view. Strangely enough, because we can't handle the intensity of depression, we start thinking about it in negative ways: "I'm no good, and my life's never going to be any good. Everybody else is living their life and having these great things happen, and here I am at the bottom of the well." This goes on and on and on.

Often, the disillusionment we feel when our dreams fall apart becomes an obsession, and people get hooked on the fact that they're not happy. For those of us who've been through terrible circumstances, sometimes the suffering itself turns into an identity, a sense that "I'm different from these other people because I've been through something they haven't, and so I understand something they don't." Being unhappy becomes a new self-image, which is just as much an ego response, and just as naive, as obsessively trying to hang on to happiness.

However, if we take depression as something to be explored, we begin to find that there are a lot of subtleties within it. If we can let go of the idea that we're depressed and simply take depression as an energy or a neutral manifestation of our life, then there's a real journey there for us. Depression is so powerful because you actually have to let go of pretty much everything you think or have thought in order to explore it. You have to let go of your hopes, your fears, your ambitions, the things that are working, the things that aren't working—your whole world. That's why depression is so powerful for spiritual practice: because if you step into it, it is actually a process of letting go of your entire known self. Few are the people who have the courage to actually do so right off the bat.

The habitual response when we hit that state of mind, the way we retain ourselves and maintain it, is by going back up into thinking. We create this whole story line around *my* depression, and *What am I going to do about it?*—and the whole thing becomes solid and self-sustaining. We use it to maintain a sense of self. But if we're willing to not go there, then the depression itself becomes this very, very powerful journey.

One of the first talks I heard my teacher Chögyam Trungpa give was on the topic of depression. He said that of all of the samsaric states—all of the ego-based states of non-enlightenment—depression is the most dignified, because it's the most real and the most accurate. You see what life really holds, ultimately. You see things as they are. You see the wishful thinking that we all indulge in all the time, and how empty and fruitless it is. Seeing the pointlessness of it all is incredibly intelligent, though it can be absolutely terrifying. Enlightenment, then, is just one little step further; instead of fighting this insight about the pointlessness of life—which is how depression maintains itself—you let go, accept it, and step into it. Then there is the most incredible feeling of relief and freedom and joy: "Wow! I am free of *myself.*" It is such a small step. When we are really depressed, we are so close.

This particular theme came up in Chögyam Trungpa's life after he had escaped the Chinese occupation in his native Tibet and was living in the United Kingdom. This happened in 1967, before he came to the United States where he became one of the main Tibetan teachers in this country. In England, he was a well educated, articulate, inspired, charismatic Tibetan monk. He radiated peacefulness and love, and was quite adored by his disciples. Unlike most other Tibetan teachers at that time, he had great respect for his Western students and wanted to offer them the full range of Tibetan teachings, including those considered the highest. For this he was severely criticized, but he stuck to his guns and kept teaching with an open hand to everyone who came to him.

Then he had a fateful stroke, and the car he was driving crashed; he was left paralyzed on one side of his body. At that point, he really didn't know what was going to happen. He got very sick because of complications related to the paralysis, and became very, very depressed. One of his students in the UK who came over to the United States with him told me about a visit that some of his disciples had made to the hospital to see him during that period. Chögyam Trungpa lay in bed with his face to the wall and was so depressed he couldn't even turn over to greet them. He was gone, because he felt like his life was over. He thought he wouldn't be able to teach again, and for him that

5

was the only purpose of his life. From that time until he came to the United States in 1970, other traumatic events, one after another, befell him, including even being expelled, by other Tibetans, from a monastery in Scotland that he had founded, and being not just attacked and criticized but vilified by his fellow countrymen, including his best friend. And all for wanting to teach the Dharma openly to Westerners. By the end of his time in the UK, he felt like he had lost everything and, according to his wife, Diana, came right to the brink of suicide.

I met him just after that period, in 1970, when he arrived in the United States. The first talk I heard him give was on depression, and it was that talk that sealed my desire to study with him, for I also had suffered greatly from depression throughout most of my twenties. He said that depression is a passage, a beautiful walkway, a walkway of the journey, of transformation, if you're willing to relate to it in the way we're talking about here—if you're willing to give up that last reference point of "poor me." That's the last shred to hang on to with depression. Are you willing to let go of "poor me, I'm the victim, I'm the least member of humanity," or whatever your approach is? Are you willing to be with the energy of it as a meditator and do what we're talking about here, which is to take your depression as your object of attending, of attention and mindfulness?

If you can be with it and look at it, then you can begin to see in the dark. If you're always looking at it from the viewpoint of the conventional world that you *think* exists, you won't be able to see; then, depression is just a black hole. But if you're willing to actually go into the depression, then you begin to be able to see in the dark, and you see that there are things going on there. There's something going on, and there's indeed a very powerful invitation—an initiation, really—to enter into the arena of death, the death of self.

Again, the reason depression is threatening is not because it is in and of itself a problematic state of mind. To reiterate, as Chögyam Trungpa pointed out, it's actually very close to the awakened state, because in the awakened state you see that ego-based, samsaric existence is absolutely hopeless and not worth living, and that there's no point in taking another step. And that's the definition of enlightenment: you see that samsara is completely unworkable, and you just don't go there anymore. Depression is so very close to that. It represents so much of the intelligence of the awakened state. And that's why people are so threatened by depression—because from the point of view of ego, enlightenment is annihilation, so that's the way we view it: as a threat.

So depression is maybe the most difficult of all the so-called "negative energies" to work with, but what is true of all of them is also true of depression: when we leave the discursive thinking behind, or at least slow it down through the practice of mindfulness, we discover all kinds of things going on in us—real things, not just thoughts—and we begin to pay attention to them. Pay attention, be with them, open to them, and just be. And then a journey starts to unfold; it's our human journey, and it's a journey that passes through many, many phases as we go, and from which we can learn so much.

For instance, depression doesn't necessarily need to involve suffering. Depression represents a certain kind of insight into the fundamental hopelessness of ordinary human life with its hopes and fears, its wishful thinking, its unrealistic ambitions to make everything easy, comfortable, and pain free. If you contemplate death deeply, if you've lost people close to you—people whom you love, people whose human face was part of your life, whose human heart nourished you and loved you—if you've lost people like that, you definitely do realize where it ends. Human life ends in the grave. That's what it all comes to, no matter what we accomplish, and if you understand that really, really deeply, depression is no problem. What we call depression is simply realizing that actually the whole thing is pretty empty and hopeless, from an ultimate point of view. Yes, short term there can be happiness, but long term, we lose everything in death.

When you land in that viewpoint and you look around, you see how phony we all are, with our little smiles on our faces, our forced cheerfulness, *no matter what,* saying, "Well, I'm happy. What's wrong? What's the problem? Everything's fine. In fact, everything is *great.* I have a great life." Often, we have somebody close to us—a parent, a sibling, a child, a friend—who is in some state of terrible emotional suffering or physical illness, or whose life is deeply tormented in some other way. But we are nevertheless determined to ignore this truth and keep that smile on our face, whatever may be going on around us. We may even seem somewhat oblivious to the very great suffering in the rest of the world. We are *that* threatened by the pain and suffering of ourselves and others.

We obviously haven't thought about things. Some of us even manage to disconnect from our actual experience in a sort of permanent way—we are permanently cheerful. This is not good. With all due respect, when we manufacture and maintain a high level of artificial cheerfulness and positivity in this way, we become among the most boring people one could ever meet. In such a state, nothing happens with us. We may even be completely numb, and when you're numb, absolutely nothing happens. There's no creativity, because creativity comes out of the unknown, groundless space of darkness—always.

That's really what we're talking about when we talk about the problem with resisting depression and other such challenging emotional states. The more beautiful life is and the more you appreciate it, the more excruciating it is, in a way, because you know that it's so fleeting. It's so fragile, and it's only just for a moment. But that kind of knowledge brings us to a path. It brings us to practice, and it inspires us to practice.

Within this context, you might say that the purpose of meditation is to learn how to relate creatively with depression and the other so-called "negative" states. Meditation, then, is not undertaken to escape the uncertainty, the fragility, and the discomfort of human life, but to enter into it more deeply. It's the recognition that if I can't force life to be what I want, then let me *let go;* and if my experience of life deepens the more I let go, then let me really understand how uncertain and fragile it all is, so I can drink in every moment of my life fully. I think that for many of us, the most excruciating thing is not really life's uncertainty and discomfort; rather, it is the sense that we're actually missing our life. We're cruising along, thinking we have a happy life, but there's some part of us that knows, *I'm missing something here. Something's not right.* Then depression can be a wake-up call for us, a teacher and a guide.

By moving beyond the preoccupation with suffering, we can see that the existence of pain and pleasure is not a problem. The fact that people get sick is not a problem. The fact that all of our dreams come to nothing is not a problem. Fundamentally, there is no problem in life, because everything that happens is actually part of the human journey and human awakening, and all of it is leading us deeper and deeper into reality. In that sense, there's no problem, even as we continue to go through these difficult mind states and experiences in the relative sense.

So, it's about opening. It's about letting go. And counterintuitive as this may seem, all of it will come through the practice of meditation, just *being with* rather than *trying to do*. That sense of the fragility, sacredness, and tenuousness of the whole thing just develops. You don't have to go looking for it—it will come to you. Because on some level, in spite of our resistance and our denial, we are already aware of it. True joy happens when you realize that you can afford to experience your life, no matter what it brings. You can afford to open to it without any reservation or judgment. You can give yourself that much latitude and that much room. That's freedom, and there's a tremendous amount of joy in that. And then you can look back at your depression and realize what a gift it was: it led you right to the door of your own deepest life; all you had to do was relate to your depression simply, directly, and nakedly, and then the door opened by itself and you found yourself just stepping right on through.

2

A Heroic Passage

James S. Gordon, MD

In pulling ourselves from the swamp of our
unhappiness, in navigating the straits of our fears
and moving beyond self-imposed limitations, in our
minds and bodies, and in our present circumstances,
we are making an effort and taking a journey that
is every bit as difficult, and as healing and heroic,
as any that humans have taken or can take.

Depression is not a disease, the end point of a pathological process. It is a sign that our lives are out of balance, that we're stuck. It's a wake-up call and the start of a journey that can help us become whole and happy, a hero's journey that can change and transform our lives.

Images of this journey have been with me for almost fifty years. Healing depression, overcoming unhappiness, means dealing more effectively with stress; recovering physical and psychological balance; reclaiming the parts of ourselves that have been ignored or suppressed; and appreciating the wholeness, the integrity, that has somehow slipped away from us, or that we have never really known. But this healing is dynamic and expansive as well as integrative, not just a series of tasks, but an adventure.

Depression almost always brings with it—along with the sense of loss and inadequacy, of gloom and uncertainty—a feeling of immobility, of stuckness. It feels as if we've broken down, alone and lonely, in some dismal, charmless backwater that no one would ever choose to visit. The beginning of the end of depression comes when we recognize this place, and see it not as the end, but a beginning, a starting point for the journey through and beyond depression and confusion and despair toward wholeness and healing and delight.

This uncertain, challenging journey is, I believe, the life-defining path which leads us to who we really are, who we are meant to be. And it is, in many ways, like the journeys that have defined our culture and the modern journeys that likewise impress and inspire us: Moses's painful pilgrimage, Jesus's mission, Mohammed's flight; the trials of confinement and the later-life challenges of contemporary heroes like Mahatma Gandhi, Senator John McCain, and Nelson Mandela; the hard-won authority of poet Maya Angelou and television teacher Oprah Winfrey; the steadfast marches of the Rev. Dr. Martin Luther King, Jr. The ancient Greek poem *The Odyssey,* the model for both our classic novels of self-discovery and our modern adventure and mystery stories, is the tale of a man "full of woe," who finally finds his way home and to wholeness.

These historic and heroic figures are taking, as mythologist Joseph Campbell, and psychiatrist Carl Jung before him, pointed out, "archetypal" journeys, journeys that reflect and embody timeless truths of human experience. Their stories can encourage us to accept, rather than flee from, the challenges that confront us, to relax with, rather than tense against, our terror. They show us that patience and courage, and awareness, creativity, and judicious action, can transform suffering. And they tell us that grace—mysterious, sweet, unmerited blessings—may always be, if we but pay attention, available. These heroes and their stories also remind us that others have been there before, that we are not alone.

The journey we take in depression—out of unhappiness—is mostly an internal one, though travel and adventure, will and action, and retreats from our customary world can also be valuable parts of it. The limitations on us, the threats to our wellbeing, our integrity, and our sanity, are not likely to be from ferocious pharaohs or sadistic jailers. They come from within ourselves; from the losses and hurt and fear we have suffered; from our internalization of the commands and constrictions—real and imagined—of our parents and our society.

These wounds and limitations manifest in our relationships to those we love and care for and work with; in the work we do and the play we permit ourselves. They are personal and, often, very private. Still, in pulling ourselves from the swamp of our unhappiness, in navigating the straits of our fears and moving beyond self-imposed limitations, in our minds and bodies, and in our present circumstances, we are making an effort and taking a journey that is every bit as difficult, and as healing and heroic, as any that humans have taken or can take.

It is this image and understanding of depression as the beginning of a journey rather than the end product of a disease process that frames the integrative approach that I bring to it.

THE CONVENTIONAL, BIOMEDICAL VIEW OF DEPRESSION

Our society and its physicians, including those who, like me, are specialists in psychiatry, treat depression as a disease. It is often compared, in both professional and popular literature, to insulin-dependent diabetes, a condition with predictable pathological findings, a strong genetic foundation, clear biochemical errors, and an obvious pharmaceutical answer. Shots of insulin are necessary to maintain adequate sugar metabolism in the diabetic, whose pancreas cannot manufacture insulin. So, the analogy goes, depressed people, whose brains cannot produce the appropriate chemicals for normal emotional functioning—neurotransmitters like serotonin and norepinephrine—require antidepressant medications.

In fact, there is no good evidence that depression is a disease in the way that insulin-dependent diabetes is. There are no consistent pathological postmortem findings in the brains of those who are depressed. The genetic association, though present, is hardly overwhelming, and a fifty-year research effort has turned up no consistent biochemical abnormalities.

There is still no proof that most people with low levels of serotonin or other neurotransmitters—or their chemical breakdown products—circulating in their blood and/or spinal fluid are depressed, nor have most depressed people been demonstrated to have low levels of such. Nor is it clear whether any such altered level of neurotransmitters might be the cause, or the consequence, of depression, or indeed what relationship it might actually have to depression. And in any case, no tests are used in clinical practice to pinpoint either those who do have lower levels of these neurotransmitters or which might be lower or, indeed, who might best respond to which antidepressant.

There is, moreover, surprisingly little evidence that the antidepressant drugs that are all but universally prescribed are more effective than a variety of other approaches—indeed more effective than the placebos, the sugar pills, to which they are compared in most scientific studies. On the other hand, there is an increasing body of information on the uncomfortable, destructive, and potentially disabling side effects of taking—and even ceasing to take—these medications.

So far as I am concerned, the narrow medical model is inappropriate and often counterproductive. The antidepressant drugs it dictates are a flawed last resort to be used only when all other approaches less burdened by side effects have failed.

AN INTEGRATIVE APPROACH TO DEPRESSION

The "treatment" that makes the most sense, for ordinary unhappiness as well as clinical depression, combines a variety of kinds of psychological guidance (including those used in cognitive and interpersonal therapy) with a number of other approaches—including exercise, meditation, guided imagery, self-expression in words, drawings, and movement, acupuncture, herbal therapies, and nutrition and supplements. Each of these techniques has been demonstrated to improve mood in significant numbers of people and to bring about physiological and, in a number of instances, anatomical brain change, without blunting the emotions or producing noxious and debilitating side effects. Each by itself may yield results that are better than placebo, and may very well be as good as, or better than, antidepressants. And many—most, really—are techniques that help us to mobilize our own capacity to help ourselves to overcome the feelings of helplessness and hopelessness—the hallmarks of depression.

Common sense urges us to consider that an approach that combines and carefully individualizes these techniques—an integrative approach—is likely to produce far better results than chemical antidepressants, at far less physical and emotional cost. This is the approach that I use, and teach, the one I bring to each stage of the journey through and beyond depression.

THE SEVEN-STAGE JOURNEY OUT OF DEPRESSION

Stage 1: The Call—Finding the Right Way

We first meet the hero of Homer's three-thousand-year-old epic *The Odyssey* sitting "in his stone seat to seaward—tear on tear / brimming his eyes." Odysseus, that brave, brilliant, richly gifted, and endlessly inventive man, is at a loss. He lives with the eternally young and beautiful goddess Kalypso. He drinks nectar and eats ambrosia by day, and makes love to her at night. It looks like a very good deal, indeed, but Odysseus, "with eyes wet / scanning the bare horizon of the sea," is miserable. He knows his destiny is elsewhere, and is immobilized, trapped, it seems forever, on Kalypso's island.

Dante Alighieri, the thirteenth-century poet, tells us, in the first lines of his *Commedia,* that he finds himself "in the middle of our life's journey . . . in a dark wood." He has "lost the right way" and feels his "heart pierced with terror."

The eight-century BC Greek hymn of Demeter begins with a pastoral scene: The young and beautiful goddess Persephone is wandering away from her companions. She pauses, gazes at a flower. Suddenly, the earth opens. Hades, the chariot-commanding dark lord of the underworld, seizes her. The earth closes over them. The scene changes. Persephone's mother, Demeter, the goddess of all that grows on earth, is blinded by tears.

One, Odysseus, apparently has everything, and is miserable; the other, Dante, is lost, disoriented, and terrified. The young goddess,

Persephone, is helplessly confined in darkness. Her mother, Demeter, is immobilized by loss. All are, though they do not yet know it, about to embark on journeys that will utterly transform their lives.

In the real time of our lives, such beginnings, such calls to change, are usually less clear and dramatic. Still, there are occasions when we realize that our world is tilting at a persistently awkward angle, mornings when we awaken to find ourselves in another country, where the colors have darkened, or bleed together.

If this is our first time, it's bound to be a shock. Disorienting anxiety piles atop depression. Why, we ask, am I feeling this way? Am I sick? Did somebody put something in my drink or food? What's going on?

Sometimes the realization comes over time, against the backdrop of a life that had seemed happy and successful. Nothing that is available or offered satisfies. We can't concentrate or finish what we've started. Day by day our steps grow heavier, and sleep becomes elusive or addictive. Enthusiasm and joy evaporate. Food and sex slowly lose their appeal. And then, one day, something happens, something that probes an old hurt in a particularly memory-evoking way or opens a new hurt, some event or feeling that grants us a new, darker perspective—and life's weight feels unbearable.

If these moments are reminders of a dark world we have for a while escaped or ignored, but which has come once again, like Hades, to claim us, we may feel doubly despairing. "Not again," we protest. "I thought I'd left that behind."

These are ordinary responses to experiencing or feeling, once again, loss and pain and disappointment. But being unhappy, even "clinically depressed," and distraught about it doesn't mean we are crazy or have a disease. Our fear, confusion, and vulnerability simply mark us as human. These dark times are a part of, not apart from, our lives. They tell us change is necessary. They call us to the journey.

Stage 2: Guides on the Journey

Even after we've recognized that we're depressed and realized we have to change, we may still be uncertain about how to do it. We may, as some books suggest, write down our emotions and sketch out steps to get where we want to go, but still feel unable to take them. Perhaps we're eating healthier foods and adding the appropriate supplements to them, and experiencing positive changes and feeling good about that. But still we want to feel even better, to make sure we're doing everything we can to move ahead.

And, no matter how determined and conscientious we are, there may be times of doubt when we feel as stuck as ever, when we cry on the shore like Odysseus, wander like Demeter in fruitless search, or tremble like Dante in the dark wood. These are signs that we need to look for and accept help, that we need to find the Guides who can support and sustain us on our journey. Odysseus had the goddess of wisdom, Athena; Dante's guide was the Roman poet Virgil; Demeter called on Hekate, goddess of the moon.

The journey through depression, beyond confusion, requires going back and forth between external and internal guidance. In the beginning, and later, too, in times of crisis and confusion, we moderns look to a human Guide, a therapist, or a teacher. He/she, like Athena, Virgil, and Hekate, holds us in the reliable healing embrace of his/her compassion and holds up to us a mirror that helps us to see and understand ourselves more fully, more generously. He/she offers us ways to deepen our understanding—perspectives, techniques, exercises, experiments—to help us to continue our journey of self-discovery outside the walls of his/her office, in every step we take.

We can learn to accept support from others as well, from professionals and friends and acquaintances, from books—and, yes, movies, music, and art, too—that offer practical advice or a larger perspective on our lives, that offer clarity and purpose, companionship and inspiration.

We can also learn to use a variety of techniques that help us to access the inner knowing that eludes rational thought and analysis. These techniques, which I describe in detail in my book *Unstuck: Your Guide to the Seven-Stage Journey Out of Depression,* include guided mental imagery, written exercises, and drawings. Guided imagery, popularized in modern times by the psychiatrist Carl Jung, is an ancient way of accessing what is variously called intuition, the imagination, the spirit, or the unconscious. After entering a relaxed state, the person is guided by a narrative that brings him/her to a safe place where he/she will meet a Wise Guide—a real or imagined person, a figure from books or scripture, an animal—who represents this unconscious wisdom. The person is then instructed to ask questions of the Guide, calling on him/her/it for advice and help. Similar access to the unconscious is achieved through drawings and through rapid, written dialogues with the problems, symptoms, or issues that may trouble or challenge us.

We can use guided imagery, drawings, and written exercises to help us develop confidence in our mind's power to explore its inner wisdom as well as control our physical and emotional functioning. As we learn to trust our inner wisdom about what's right for us—our own Wise Guidance—we're able to measure what we're learning and feeling with our Outer (Wise) Guide and in the rest of our life against the images and answers that arise from within. We'll be able to find answers to problems that had seemed insoluble, ways to lift our mood that we'd forgotten or never before imagined. Little by little, as we keep on using the Inner Guide imagery, this inner knowing, which will become the surest and most enduring of all our Guides, will grow stronger and stronger.

Stage 3: Surrender to Change

Often "surrendering," or letting go of control, is necessary to move us ahead on our journey. Surrender isn't the same as submission. Submission means giving up, resigning ourselves to the limitations that are holding us back or keeping us down. In surrendering, we're opening ourselves up to the current of our life, which is always moving, always changing. And we're inviting and embracing the deep changes that are starting to work inside of us. Sometimes, for some of us, surrender may happen easily, with little effort. More often, surrender requires exertion. We have to act consciously to free ourselves from the places where we're stuck before we can relax into the new freedom we're discovering.

Exercise—movement—is often the most effective door to surrender. Movement alters brain chemistry and, with it, mood. Thirty to forty minutes of daily exercise—jogging, biking, swimming, lifting weights, using the StairMaster or treadmill, walking—reliably raises the levels of serotonin and norepinephrine, the two neurotransmitters that most antidepressants aim at increasing, as well as endorphins, the brain's pain-reducing and pleasure-enhancing amino acid peptides. Exercise likely increases the number and activity of neurons in the hippocampus that are depleted in depression and seem to be so important to emotional wellbeing. In study after study, exercise (jogging has been most studied) decreases people's depression scores, sometimes by as much as 50 percent, a result fully as good as that obtained by psychotherapy or chemical antidepressants. If exercise were a patentable and profitable pill, it would be hailed on the front pages of every American newspaper, and marketed 24/7 on television networks.

All movement can be helpful, but the expressive meditations that have been developed in traditional societies are freeing as well as energizing, breaking up the fixed, stuck emotional and physical patterns that constrain us when we are depressed, allowing us to be present to, healed by, the continuous change that is the real nature of life and of our lives. The experiential technique I use most often begins with shaking our body and concludes with dancing. Shaking may require a bit of a leap of faith—we may feel that shaking is an undesirable sign of anxiety and fear, or that doing it is silly. It may also seem like too much when we're feeling fatigued, fatalistic, and down. We need to put aside our preconceptions to accept, at least provisionally, that even if it is arduous and/or silly, it may help shake loose some of the chronic tension that restricts and agitates us. If we do, we may well find, as have thousands of people with whom I've done this meditation, that this paired sequence of activities can energize the depressed body, relieve the preoccupied mind, and dissolve tension. It can also, as we do it regularly, help us feel more at home in our bodies and surrender into the moment-to-moment flow of our lives.

Stage 4: Dealing with Demons

All of us have ways of thinking, feeling, and being that inhibit and constrain us, difficulties we avoid, and addictive, self-defeating habits that fuel our avoidance. Borrowing from Buddhist psychology, I call these patterns "demons." They may contribute in significant ways to our chronic, low-grade dissatisfaction and unhappiness. As we move forward on our journey through depression, these "demons" (guilt, pride, perfectionism, loneliness, lethargy, resentment, etc.) may rise to confront and challenge us with painful, frightening force.

Modern biological psychiatry regards the intimidating patterns and terrors of depression not as demons, but as symptoms of a disease. It responds by attempting to mute, deny, and obliterate these symptoms, using drugs to take the edge off sufferers's pain, quiet their fears, deny their doubts, and focus them elsewhere. This is understandable but shortsighted, and often proves counterproductive, even destructive. Demons denied will keep returning, often with heightened fury. And by trying to suppress them, we also lose the wisdom they bear.

It is my experience—and one of the fundamental insights of both the modern depth psychology of Freud and Jung, and the ancient wisdom of Buddhism—that the demons that terrify us are those parts of ourselves, of our history, and of life that we have feared, hated, and denied. To heal and become whole, we need to confront, acknowledge, and accept the demons, and to take back the power we have yielded to them.

We have the choice to listen and be steadfast, to act and be aware, and to not react. This meditative state is the best posture for confronting, learning from, and taking on the power of all the forces that would constrain, undermine, and depress us.

In this relaxed, aware state, we can use a variety of techniques to mobilize our imagination to help us to learn the lessons our demons have to teach us: drawings of what troubles us most and of how we might respond to it; dialogues with the demons who often turn out, to our surprise, to be Guides; consultations with our Wise Guide that can become an ongoing part of our journey. Demons may arise at any time. The hero's way teaches us to recognize, accept, and learn from, rather than avoid or deny, them.

Stage 5: The Dark Night of the Soul

There may be a time at the beginning of, or later on in, our journey when any of us may feel overwhelmed, despondent, or despairing. Sometimes the cause of our despair—our loss of hope—is expected and obviously devastating: e.g., the sudden death of someone we love or a diagnosis that predicts terrible suffering or imminent death. Sometimes it feels as if we've lost ground gained with great pain, slipped back downhill. We've failed at another attempt to break an old, persistent addiction, or a spouse or lover or friend or Guide we'd counted on has disappointed or disappeared. Sometimes we say to ourselves, "I can't go on" or "I'd be better off dead."

This stage on the journey, this Dark Night, shares some of the characteristics of the first one, the Call. There is, in both, confusion and recognition of distress and disturbance, a sense that prior efforts at understanding and problem-solving have failed. And, indeed, this kind of Dark Night can signal the beginning of the journey. But it is, as its name suggests, different, too—deeper, darker, more laden with despair.

Still, there is also something deeply hopeful about the Dark Night of the Soul. Dark Nights, by definition, are finite. They are part of a natural process of change and progression, and they yield, inevitably, to brighter mornings.

Indeed, many aboriginal societies—from the Plains Indians to African forest dwellers—choose to make a Dark Night experience a part of the growth and healing of its members, a rite of passage to adulthood. Sometimes, as in the healing temples of ancient Greece, this kind of immersion in darkness is a crucial element in the healing of serious illness, including depression. In many societies, future healers are marked out by their successful, early-life encounter with the unavoidable Dark Night of a life-threatening illness, a psychosis, or suicidal despair.

The Homeric hymn of Demeter and Persephone is, as psychologist Thomas Moore points out, particularly relevant to these Dark Nights. The Dark Night's ideal guide is Hekate, witch and healer and goddess of the moon. Hekate alone hears Persephone's cry. In the underworld,

Hekate comes to Persephone, as well as to her mother, Demeter, who is wandering distraught aboveground. Hekate brings news back and forth between despairing daughter and frantic mother, and wisdom, too: separation and loneliness, darkness and despair, are inevitable; healing and wholeness come only when we accept such things as part of—not apart from—our lives.

Very few of us can move through these Dark Nights alone and without guidance. Friends who are steadfast, unafraid, matter of fact, and loving can be of great help, but most of us also need a professional Guide who honors and is at ease in the darkest places. He/she comforts and reassures us by his/her presence and gives us pause and much-needed perspective. Our connection with him/her builds a bridge back to life, over which his/her words and gestures—sometimes warm, sometimes sharp, always understanding—help us walk.

Stage 6: Spirituality—The Blessing

Just about everyone who makes the journey out of depression feels, sooner or later, a connection to something larger than himself/herself that touches and transforms his/her life. Both this connection and that larger "something" are what we often call "spiritual."

The word *spirit* is in many languages—Sanskrit, Hebrew, and Greek among them—identical with, or closely connected to, the word for breath. We define the beginning and end of our lives by the breaths we take. Breathing connects what is most vital within us to the world beyond our brain and body. And breathing is fundamental to meditation, which can open the door to the spiritual dimension.

Prayer affirms our connection to the spiritual. Faith and hope give us courage when we feel separated from it. And forgiveness is good for breaking down the barriers—the resentment, hurt, anger, and fear—we have erected against it. But love is, of all our experiences, the one that most consistently allows us to live in and with the spiritual.

When we are feeling terribly discouraged about ourselves, the love of another is literally wonderful: full of wonder. It is as if the sun has suddenly risen in the middle of the Dark Night. We see more clearly, feel warmed, and move about more freely. But the happiness, the ful-fillment, rarely lasts "ever after."

The love of others cannot ultimately sustain us. If we haven't changed what made us depressed—the imbalances and distortions that our demons cause, the unmet needs and unfulfilled potential—we will eventually drain the other's love of its healing force and warp it to fit our still-crippled form. We will, in short, repeat more or less the same patterns, with more or less the same depressing consequences.

The love that heals us, that allows us to let ourselves be loved and to love ourselves, is of a different kind. This love is at once lyrical and intimate, elevating, demanding, and practical. It requires demonstra-tion on a daily—actually, minute-by-minute—basis.

Meditation, which quiets our nervous systems and allows us to more calmly confront our demons, may open the door to love. Relaxing, becoming aware of and accepting of whatever we experience—inter-esting thoughts and "foolish" ones, good feelings and bad, fears and insecurities, and arrogance as well as kindness—is a kind of love for us as we are, with all our imperfections.

Meditative practice helps us to become aware that we have a choice—to open up to and embrace our experience rather than pro-tect ourselves against it. So many of depression's demons are forms of self-protection. Perfectionism keeps us from being wrong, and pro-crastination, from failing or being hurt or moving on and ahead. Envy and resentment separate us from the one against whom we've devel-oped a grudge, and feeling lonely certifies our isolation. When we eventually allow ourselves to appreciate what we've protected ourselves against, we are moving into the current of life, experiencing an expan-siveness that is very much like love.

Love also comes as a grace, and sometimes when we least expect it—through a romantic relationship when we are ready for it, or friendship, or, and perhaps most often for adults, through children. The connection to a child—Odysseus's to his son, Telemachus, Deme-ter's to Persephone—can open our hearts more widely than we had ever imagined; sustain us like life's blood through the darkest of nights; transform us in ways that we may find astonishing.

Stage 7: The Return

The time after we've moved through depression, when its weight is lifting and leaving us, is a time for celebration. We should savor the sights and sounds and movement of these days and weeks, as if we've just come out of a cave in which we've been trapped. Each glimpse of the bright world can awaken our eyes.

During this time, we also need to be relaxed and mindful, to hold our good feelings lightly, with gratitude and grace. When I think of the return after the journey through and beyond depression, I think of obstacles overcome and wisdom and peace obtained: Odysseus vanquishing the suitors and reuniting with his wife; Dante, having moved through the Inferno, rising through the Purgatorio to the Paradiso; Demeter and Persephone together again.

I also remember stories from around the world in which the hero—dissatisfied, despondent, perhaps even despairing—sets off to find the priceless jewel or the peerless bride. He travels long and far, overcoming countless obstacles, only to return home to discover that the jewel was sitting on his windowsill; that the ideal bride all along had lived next door. The scene of our lives may or may not be different, but as we come to the close of this part of our journey out of depression, we have new eyes with which to see it.

3

Ingenious Stagnation

Karla McLaren, MEd

> Depression arises to tell you when things have
> gone awry, and it stops you from moving forward.
> Depression derails you, certainly, but what I learned
> from conversing with depression is that it derails you
> for a reason. Something somewhere has gone wrong,
> and depression's job is to slow you down or even stop
> you completely so that you can attend to it.

I've learned over a lifetime that all emotions are messengers that bring gifts, skills, and vital information. All emotions have meaning and purpose, and even depression, that troubling and unwanted condition—even depression has gifts for you. I'd like to introduce you to these gifts, because depression is actually a friend of mine. Depression and I grew up together; we learned language together, experienced trauma and abuse together, and walked hand in hand through life together. Depression has kept me company through some of the hardest times in my life, and it has called to me and listened to me—awake to all words, all situations, all dreams, all hopes, and all losses. Through all this, depression has become an old, old friend of mine.

Of course, depression didn't always feel so friendly. I've experienced three varieties of depression (each of us has a different experience of depression, and depression has many forms). As a young child, I lived with a mild form of depression called *dysthymia,* which for me involved a steady low mood that was my constant companion, lots of sadness and grief, and intermittent bursts of anger and rage. Though mild dysthymia did have its downsides, it also contributed a richly dark worldview, a piercingly accurate bullshit detector, and a deliciously dark sense of humor. As a child, I learned how to work with my dysthymia; we were friends.

I also learned how to work with another form of depression that is now called *situational depression*, or a low mood and a loss of energy that (if you can turn toward it and take inventory of your situation) tracks directly to upheavals in your life: in your health, your relationships, or your work life. Once I learned how to listen to what this form of depression was trying to say, I found that situational depression was also my friend; it had a message and a purpose, and there was something I could do to relieve it once I understood what had evoked it. With the help of situational depression, I learned how to take a full inventory of my life and my situation, and to identify where things had gone awry. When I addressed these problems, situational depression would lift; it responded logically and respectfully to my efforts. It was my companion and my friend.

But a third form of depression didn't seem to be my friend at all. My first severe depressive episode arose when I was ten years old, and it was all I could do to hold myself together while intense darkness and despair whirled through and around me. I somehow made it through, and this new form of depression (which is now called *major* or *clinical depression*), this new constellation of emotions (some hyperactivated, some strangely silent), followed by extreme darkness and then a quiet, exhausted emotionlessness—this new version of depression soon became a part of my life. Sometimes, these severe depressive episodes would last for a day or two, or sometimes they'd drag out for a week or longer. They came and went randomly, and they occurred on a timetable that had some sort of internal logic, though it wasn't one I could decode. These episodes didn't seem to have any friendly intentions whatsoever. They would reach up and drag me into the underworld, and keep me there until they were done with me.

I learned how to survive these episodes, often by scaring myself out of suicide with thoughts of failing at it and being incapacitated, and sometimes by imagining that suicide would be punished by some spiritual force, or that I would be compelled to reincarnate and go through life again, except in worse circumstances. Unlike with my other forms of depression, I couldn't make sense of these severe episodes, and they didn't seem to contribute anything at all; they seemed only to take. I couldn't figure out how the episodes fit together, and I couldn't understand their narrative arc. One day I was fine, and bam, the next I was in the underworld, barely surviving. I learned how to exist in the spaces between these tempests of major depression, but I wished fervently that they would go away. This form of depression was *not* my friend.

I hid my depression; of course, I did. In the middle-class neighborhood where I grew up, very few emotions were openly welcomed. People expected obedience, shallow conversations, smiling faces, and no questions about the monsters that often hid behind those faces. In a community where emotions besides happiness and a little bit of sadness weren't welcomed, I was surrounded by emotional subterfuge. There was so little emotional honesty or clarity around me. Most emotions were ignored or repressed, and emotions that were openly obvious were often shamed outright. Anger, openly expressed, was treated as a loss of control. Sadness, deeply expressed, was treated as weakness. Fear, too—and grief, and shame, and pretty much every emotion except that old standby, happiness. But even with happiness, you could only express a certain amount; too much happiness was, like anger, also treated as a loss of control. I learned very early that emotions were mostly to be avoided.

Depression, of course, was especially unwelcome. Depression was treated as a character flaw and a moral failing. Depression was a disease, a private shame, and a catastrophic loss of face. Depression was not simply something to be avoided; it was something to be shunned. So, of course, I hid my depression. But as most of us learn sooner or later, avoiding emotions (especially depression) isn't really possible.

Before I learned to befriend my major-depressive episodes, to pay attention to them, to speak to them, and to listen closely to their messages, I blamed them for ruining my life. I thought that everything would be perfect if my detestable depressive episodes would just go away. Dysthymia was workable (and frankly comforting), and situational depression was valuable, but these major-depressive episodes were just gruesome. As a highly empathic person, I had learned in my teens how to empathize directly with emotions, how to speak to and receive messages from all of them—from the Honorable Sentry of Anger, from the Water Bearer of Sadness, from the Intuitive Genius of Fear, and so forth—and I had become a friend to all of them . . . but I avoided speaking to my intense depression because it was such a ghastly and destructive force in my life. I was afraid to speak to it, and doubly afraid to hear what it had to say.

But one day when I was in my late twenties, a severe depressive episode became so severe that I finally gathered the courage to turn toward it and yell, "*What?* What do you want from me?" I steeled myself for what I was certain would come: a shrieking litany of my faults, my inadequacies, and my failures. But none of that happened.

Instead, I suddenly saw in my mind's eye a scene, like in a movie, and I understood that it was a message from my severe depression. What I saw was the city of London in World War II, gray and devastated, bombed-out buildings standing next to homes and businesses—a city shattered by war. As I watched the scene unfold, I saw parents awash in grief, fear, and desperation as they packed their children's belongings and sent them away to safety, to relatives and friends who lived in the country.

I saw that my severe depression was acting in much the same way those parents were. It was sending those children (who symbolized my energy, my hope, my capacity for pleasure, and my future) away from imminent danger for their own protection. I write about this scene in the depression chapter in my book *The Language of Emotions: What Your Feelings Are Trying to Tell You* (Sounds True, 2010), and draw on those passages here.

This image told me that the depression was not attacking me but sending parts of my soul away to safety while it held fast in a combat zone. This was a shock—and it had nothing whatsoever to do with anything I had ever been told about depression. There was a definite and palpable protective movement occurring inside me—not a disability or a lunacy, but a decisive and conscious maneuver made by a part of me I hadn't known existed until that moment. Suddenly, with the help of that previously unrecognized aspect of myself, I was able to observe my other emotions, fighting to be heard over my internal din—struggling, gasping, and dying—as my depression worked desperately to save my life. I most especially felt the anger trapped beneath my depression, anger that wasn't able to protect me or restore my ravaged boundaries, but was instead reduced to making agonizing, stopgap decisions in the face of tragedy.

I have since discovered the origin of the war my psyche was fighting so grimly—and why the children of my soul had to be sent away for their own safety. At the time, I was still running on the fumes of trauma, dissociation, emotional suppression, and massive internal clashes (I had survived years of childhood sexual assault when I was a toddler). However, since I had learned (as most of us do) to gloss over and work around all my internal troubles, I no longer had clear awareness of them. In fact, I actually looked fairly good on the outside—pretty functional—except for my detestable, unrelenting depression. In my opinion, depression was the only thing wrong with me; if it would just go away, I'd be happy and well. But the vision my severe depression presented shook me out of my complacent, repressive trance—because its depiction of a world at war was piercingly and inarguably accurate. When I was able to reframe my view of myself with the support of that vision, I marveled that I could feel anything *but* depression, because my psyche had become a full-scale battle zone. The crippling lack of energy, focus, peace, and happiness I experienced in my depression wasn't the problem, and it didn't arise by mistake or by accident; my energy was depleted because some part of me had sent it away on purpose—to keep it safe and alive until the end of my war.

I have since observed a similar situation in each case of depression I've encountered in others (though the components and intensity are unique to each person). Something sentient in the soul reacts to extreme internal or external instability by hiding energy in outlying areas until the center of the soul is habitable and capable of conscious action.

If you can take hold of this analogy, it can help you remove the taint of pathology from your own movements into depression. Rather than seeing yourself as an incompetent or destroyed person, you can bring compassion to your struggle and essentially roll up your sleeves and get to work—instead of being worked over. You can discover the logic behind your depression, which will help you see that no healthy forward movement can or should be undertaken from a position of strife and instability (you can't make coherent decisions or take effective actions if elements inside you are trying to murder each other!). Instead of fighting a futile, repressive battle that will only intensify your internal strife, you can honor your depression's inhibiting tactics; you can tune in to your depression and listen to its wisdom. Though this is a very necessary healing step, it is a difficult step to take in a culture that urges you to soldier ever onward instead of stopping to reflect upon the situations you have faced and the direction your life has taken.

Unfortunately, our modern culture does not value reflection—which means that the soul-rescuing essence of depression is not readily accessible. Instead, depression has been desecrated and pathologized—while our ability to address internal and external injustice has consequently deteriorated. If you agree to demonize depression, you won't be able to truly alleviate it, no matter what you do. You'll have few skills, impaired emotional agility, and no true grasp of what is occurring in your psyche or your world. But if you can create sacred space and protect yourself from the deluded beliefs careering through our culture, you can perform the soul-honoring and life-saving tasks your depression asks of you.

The honorable task of depression isn't to get happy, nor is it merely to restore your lost energy (or crank up your existing energy), because these emotionally repressive approaches cannot in any way address the original imbalance that initiated your depression in the first place. Repressive techniques may erase your depression in the short run, but in the long run, where do they leave you? Do you have more skills or internal resources? Are you fully upright and emotionally competent? Or are you merely less depressed? Depression exists for a specific and protective reason, and it is not the enemy. It is not the creator of the war inside you, and it isn't even one of the combatants. Depression has the thankless task of restricting your energy when an internal (or external) war has already started, and it grimly and deliberately impedes your ability to walk down the wrong path doing the wrong thing with the wrong intention.

Your soulful task is not to erase your depression and keep walking; it is to understand your necessary movements into stagnation and to address your depression as a peer instead of as a combatant. Your sacred task is to end the war inside you, clear away the rubble, restore the flow in your internal kingdom, and make a home the children of your soul would want to come back to.

I call depression *Ingenious Stagnation,* because it always stops you for a reason, whether it has to do with your health, your biochemistry, your emotional regulation skills, your relationships, your work life, your surroundings, difficulties in your past, or your hopes for the future—there is always a reason. Depression can be a natural protective response to disheartening or destabilizing situations, and the sacred task in the realm of depression is not to magically become undepressed, as if depression is the problem in and of itself. No. The task is to turn toward the depression (with support), converse with it, listen to its message, and discover where the issues lie.

Turning toward my severe depression literally saved my life. And while depressions of this magnitude can and do destabilize your health and wellbeing (thankfully, there are therapists, doctors, and counselors who can help stabilize you), depression always points to real trouble in some aspect of your life. Depression arises to tell you when things have gone awry, and it stops you from moving forward. Depression derails you, certainly, but what I learned from conversing with depression is that it derails you for a reason. Something somewhere has gone wrong, and depression's job is to slow you down or even stop you completely so that you can attend to it. Depression has a purpose and a message for you. Depression is not a character flaw or a sign of moral failing. Depression has a purpose.

I call depression Ingenious Stagnation because when you can work with your depression and really listen to it, it can tell you absolutely life-changing things about situations that affect you deeply, even (and especially) if you have been avoiding and ignoring those situations. This kind of no-holds-barred truth-telling is what a real friend, a deep and abiding friend, will do for you. Depression can be your friend.

Of course, depression can become very serious, and many forms of depression require therapeutic and/or medical attention. Mine certainly did, because even though I learned how to work directly with my depression and listen to what it had to say, I had spent too many years in untreated and unaddressed depression. Current research is suggesting that untreated depression, especially major-depressive episodes like mine, can essentially teach your brain how to fall into depression more easily the next time. Even situational depression, if it is not addressed and attended to mindfully, can lead to more serious forms of depression. Depression has a purpose, which is to tell you that something is wrong. Your job is to find out what that something is and address it—or to reach out for help if you can't figure things out on your own. Untreated depressions can almost wear a path in your brain, so it's very important to address depression with whatever supports and therapies best suit your particular situation.

In my empathic work with emotions, I teach people to ask questions of their emotions. Each emotion has a unique purpose and a unique question, and for depression, the questions are these:

> *Where has my energy gone?*
> *Why was it sent away?*

Notice that these questions have nothing to do with failure or character flaws, and nothing to do with cheering people up. Instead, these questions treat depression as a valid emotional state that contains useful information.

With my own depression (situational or major), I've learned to walk through a kind of life inventory: I check in with my health, my diet and exercise, my home environment, and my sleep. I check in with my relationships with my family, my friends, and my colleagues. I check in with my work life, my finances, and my career path. I look at my community, my political environment, and issues of human rights and social justice. In essence, I take an account of my life and ask my depression to point out where the problems are. Sometimes, I need to work with a friend or counselor to figure out the entire situation that brought my depression forward, but I've learned to treat my depression as a vital message about serious problems—instead of mistakenly treating depression as the problem itself.

I've also learned to look at depression sociologically, because so much focus in depression alleviation is placed on us: on our behaviors, our chemistry, or our habits of thought. But depression isn't merely an internally generated emotion; often, depression is a response to external trouble. For instance, conflicts, difficulties, abuse, injustice, illness, loss, and upheaval—these things *should* evoke some depression.

In the face of troubles, something in us should stop moving blithely forward as if nothing is happening. Something in us should drop, lose energy, and experience a sense of despair or hopelessness every now and then. Depression can be very problematic, it's true, and we should be vigilant about how long we maintain a depressive mood, but depression also has a purpose, and it contains ingenious information that can help us through difficult times.

Depression can lead us into the dark night of the soul, but it can also lead us through that night and into the dawn of new ideas, new possibilities, and a deeper understanding of what it is to be fully and deeply human. Depression can be our friend—if only we can learn how to listen to it.

4

Despair Cracks Open Our Hearts

An Interview with Mary Pipher, PhD

Most of us forget to notice when our hearts are swelling with joy and we forget to notice when our hearts are aching in sorrow. That particular piece of body awareness is immensely valuable to orient ourselves toward what we need to be doing right now to heal and be in a healthier place.

Tami Simon   Can you describe your view of depression, speaking from your own experience?

Mary Pipher   I'm more comfortable talking about "despair" than "depression," because I'm not fond of the ways depression has been bracketed by pharmaceutical companies and the mental-health profession. It sounds as if we're talking about pathology, about something that spares a good part of the human race. When I was in my fifties, I switched from using psychological language to using Buddhist language because the more I read about depression, the more damaged I felt. I felt damaged and unique, as if I were a list of symptoms and neuroses. When I switched to reading Buddhism, I stopped feeling damaged immediately and I felt something much different—I felt human. I felt that I was a member of a human race of seven billion people who suffer and that, like everyone else, to avoid suffering I would need to learn some skills. In my view, despair is prevalent, if not universal. It's a more interesting word to discuss then depression and a more fascinating existential state to ponder.

Despair happens when our inner and outer resources are not sufficient to cope with the world as we're experiencing it. Our traditional ways of coping stop working, so the confidence we have—that if we do this or that we'll be okay, that if we follow our habitual patterns things will work out okay for us—all of this disappears when we feel despair.

I also think that despair is a disruption of trust—our own trust in the universe and in our own capacity to deal with that universe. We no longer trust that the way we do things, the way that we see the world, will help us move forward. During the moments that we're flailing, we lose trust in the idea that the universe is kind enough to hold us up until we recover. All of us have times in our lives when terrible things happen and that's when, without faith in our resilience and without a belief that the universe is ultimately kind, we can go to dark places.

In my own experience of despair, it has been helpful to have a spiritual path. Because one way to think of despair is: our problems have grown too big for us to handle. The solution to that particular problem is for us to each grow bigger, which means a spiritual transformation. It means moving into what I call a "transcendent response"—connecting to something much larger than ourselves.

TS   Can you share more about your own experience moving through despair and how engaging a spiritual path helped you in your journey? Was trust restored for you?

MP   I have had many a crisis of confidence in myself. In *Seeking Peace,* I describe one such point during my career as a writer. I was extremely lucky—my writing career was a Cinderella story because I went from being an ordinary therapist in Lincoln, Nebraska, to being a *New York Times* bestseller. However, that "luck" required that I travel constantly, speak in front of large crowds, and live in hotel rooms.

After seven years of this, I had a meltdown while I was on the road. I was tired, I had a cold, it was November, airplanes were breaking down, and I was just worn out: traveling too much, far away from people who loved me, distanced from the natural world, my cats, my home, and my own nourishing food. I hit a wall. I knew I was in trouble when my husband and I went into a little café we would never have stopped at otherwise, but we were hungry and on the way to a speaking engagement. We needed to eat. It was a dirty-looking place and I'd been reading *Fast Food Nation* on the plane. I ordered a bowl of chili. When it arrived, I tasted it and said to my husband, "This chili tastes like shit." He looked at me as if I was crazy and I realized that either I was eating chili that had fecal matter in it and that's why it tasted like shit to me, or I was so down and blue that I was imagining it. At that moment, I said to my husband, "I want to go home. I need to get off the road and I need to stop doing this to myself for a while, until I can build my strength back."

We did go home, and I spent three or four months that winter resting, reading a lot of Buddhism, cooking vegetable soup, reading history, and taking long walks in the snow with my friends. That rest was deeply nutritious in every sense of the word, a deeply healing experience.

But I also realized I had work to do on myself. I had always been someone who pushed through pain and discomfort and showed up present, with a smile on my face and a hard-working, cheerful attitude. I created a theory, when I was young, that if I was a good girl and pleasing all the time, the world would work just fine. I had to face that myth and the fact that it was destroying me. I needed to change. That was the beginning of meditating and working more on self-awareness, developing curiosity about myself, and shedding judgment. It has been a long process: I continue to go to Buddhist retreats and read books. I have continued to work on my schedule and develop ways to be more honest and nurturing with myself.

TS   You speak of despair as a universal experience, and I'm wondering if you think despair plays some type of role, or has some type of purpose, in the psyche?

MP   Oh, absolutely. Despair is a healthy response to reality in 2014 and to the general tragedies of life. In addition, we move around the world filled with opinions, self-perceptions, and stories about ourselves and other people. At some point we're confronted with a bigger truth we cannot deny. At that point, despair can be a way to break through, to achieve transcendence. Many people say that their worst moment turned out to be their best moment, because, in their times of crises, despair cracked open their hearts. When our hearts crack open, we also feel joy and we wake up.

The mental state before despair can be a numbness to the world and to one's own experience: a deadening of the heart, a deadening of the sensory life, because the signals are too threatening to allow.

One of the important things about despair is that no experience is wasted if you learn something from it. You can look back on a dark night of the soul and say, "Because of that suffering, I'm a stronger person, or a kinder person, or a more connected person, or a more spiritual person. That dark night of the soul was a good thing."

TS   Often when people report being in despair or being depressed, they describe repetitive thought loops that go on in their heads, a type of endless rumination over the same depressive ideas. What might help people when they find themselves in this state?

MP   I have those repetitive thought loops; I'm very familiar with them. The main antidote is self-awareness, so that you can catch yourself in those thought loops. There's an urban legend about a psychoanalyst who would sit listening to people for hours at a time, and then periodically would hold up a card that he'd had printed and laminated. It said, "Yours is the saddest story I have ever heard." We *all* think we have the saddest story ever told, and his intervention was actually very funny, because when patients would see the sign they would realize their cognitive misperceptions about themselves and also the fact that everybody has those same, crazy misperceptions. That card worked on everybody.

We can all engage negative self-talk, problem-saturated stories, feelings of being victims of our own life, and so on. Recently, I encountered a beautiful poem by Thich Nhat Hanh called "Our True Heritage." The poem is celebrating joy: the joy of breathing, of the pines chanting with wind, the flowers blooming, and so on. And here's the line that, in this context, really struck me:

> You, the richest person on earth,
> who have been going around begging for a living,
> stop being the destitute child.
> Come back and claim your heritage.

The poem reminds us of what a beautiful heritage we have with the earth and the skies. I use the line, "Stop being the destitute child," as a kind of a skillful tool to pull myself back into gratitude.

Another element of despair is that we stop loving ourselves. Because most of us are our own tormenters and our own grand inquisitors, unless we deal with our own inner harsh critic, the inner hanging judge, we can't heal from despair. Instead, we continue to inflict despair upon ourselves. So to move beyond despair, we want to learn to cherish ourselves. I do this by being outdoors or with people I love, reading and listening to music. Cherishing ourselves is medicine.

TS   You spoke of your experience of becoming physically depleted and despairing as a result of success. You work with refugees and other people who have had such great losses in their lives, and your despair came as a result of worldly success. I'm curious how you were able to be kind to yourself, thinking, "Here's the saddest story in the world: I'm making lots of money and have invitations to speak all over the world."

MP   Actually, that contributed to the depression because I felt so guilty for not being happy. I had things that everybody I knew wanted. I've lived an extraordinarily lucky life and I'm very grateful for it. But despair is not a cognitive state; despair is an emotional state, and it perceives life from a very different level than thoughts.

For example, for years while I was telling myself, "I am happy," "I am lucky," "I am doing just great," "I am extremely productive," my body was telling me something totally different. My blood pressure was very high, I had terrible insomnia, I lost my appetite and a lot of weight. By the time I stopped being on the road, I was a very agitated person. I said to a friend, "You know, I'm really theoretically very happy." And she said, "You can't be theoretically happy any more than you can be theoretically angry." I realized then that I was not happy. I was telling myself I should be happy.

One of the things I am careful never to do is to compare my despair with the despair of others. Despair is universal. I'm reading a wonderful new biography about Johnny Cash, and by most accounts he was an extraordinarily successful man. But his life was filled with despair, and never more so than when he was at the top of his game in terms of celebrity, fame, and red-hot records. It's very common for people who are doing well to be filled with despair, because their lives are changing so rapidly and they're often pulled far from what feels safe, familiar, and comforting. I'll give you another example of this business of despair not being cognitive. There's an old poem by Edwin Arlington Robinson called "Richard Cory."

Whenever Richard Cory went down town,
We people on the pavement looked at him:
He was a gentleman from sole to crown,
Clean favored, and imperially slim.

And he was always quietly arrayed,
And he was always human when he talked;
But still he fluttered pulses when he said,
"Good-morning," and he glittered when he walked.

And he was rich—yes, richer than a king—
And admirably schooled in every grace:
In fine, we thought that he was everything
To make us wish that we were in his place.

So on we worked, and waited for the light,
And went without the meat, and cursed the bread;
And Richard Cory, one calm summer night,
Went home and put a bullet through his head.

Richard Cory has everything: money, charm, good looks, popularity, but he still put a bullet through his head. No matter how a person looks on the outside, no matter how objectively we think we can evaluate their life via a checklist of accomplishments, we never know what a person is experiencing. As a therapist, I would see people who had, on one level, such beautiful lives that the feeling was, "Well, how dare you not to be happy? You have a wonderful husband and an interesting career and tons of people who love you." The emotional pain of their lives was beyond their cognitive control, and it was in their body and it was in their heart.

Being grateful is a skill that we all need to learn. For example, when I have a really strong moment of despair, one of the things I try to do is find something beautiful. So I read a poem, I play a beautiful piece of music, I look out the window with binoculars until I see a bird. That's a skill; it's not a character trait or the result of circumstance. We are all entitled to experience the whole gamut of human emotion, and we all experience [these emotions] in different ways. Certainly, people living in war zones are suffering on a level we can barely imagine. But the Buddha was right when he said, "Life is suffering." Most of us experience that as part of the human condition.

TS   You mentioned that your guilt about being fortunate contributed to your sense of despair. Can you say more about this?

MP   For me, guilt is inside my despair. I tend to cut other people a lot of slack—but I don't offer any to myself. I criticize myself for not being as polite and kind as I think I should be. So guilt has always been something I've had to work hard at overcoming.

One of the ways I deal with it is to do what one of the great Buddhist teachers instructs: to hug myself and say, "Darling, I love you just the way you are." Doing that always makes me laugh. The other thing I do is say a prayer for all the people like me. For example, say I get irritated with my husband and snap at him. Later, when I feel angry at myself, I say a prayer for all the women in the world who've ever been snappy and irritable with their mates. When I say a prayer for all the people like myself, I find it much easier to open up my heart to myself. Because I bear those other people no ill will, I can easily forgive them. When I do that, I open my heart to myself as well.

TS   You said that, in your view, despair is not so much a cognitive as it is an emotional process. Some people might say that the emotional process is also a physical process.

MP   Oh, it's absolutely physical! These strange divides we make in the Western world don't really exist: body, mind, emotions, thoughts—they're all more interactive and synergistic than our ways of talking suggest. For example, before 2001, I'd never had a massage—I just didn't feel comfortable with a stranger touching my body. But in that hard winter, I was so jittery and tense that I decided to try it. I started feeling more peaceful emotionally because massage calmed down my body. I'd rush into my massage stressed and tensed and worrying about if I should even be there, and after an hour I would feel so much better about my life. I worked on body awareness. Most of my life I had put aside my own needs and ignored all kinds of bodily signals about being uncomfortable, in pain, or tired. I also started doing yoga, which is another way to rapidly feel one's body. I love swimming, and I find it helps me with an upset mind. Swimming is rhythmic and its movements are tied to breathing. It is one of the most beautiful and pleasant ways to work with the body.

As body awareness comes, we all can learn to experience, literally, the sensations in our hearts. We can pay attention to them as opposed to overriding them with cognitions. My little granddaughter once turned to me and said, "Nana, my heart feels very big." I asked what she meant by that, and she said, "Well, Nana, my heart feels full; it feels full like my stomach would feel full." She could feel her heart swelling with joy. Most of us forget to notice when our hearts are swelling with joy or aching in sorrow. That particular piece of body awareness is valuable [for orienting] ourselves toward what we need to be doing right now to heal and be in a healthier place.

TS   In your life as a writer, have you seen a relationship between the act of writing, of engaging the world as a writer, and the experience of despair?

MP   Writing is a wonderful way to cope with despair, because writing allows us to reflect on experience, to explore it, and to reframe it, which can be a very healing, transformative process. Many writers will say that it is what saved them; they would not be alive without it. Simply getting something out of one's brain and onto a piece of paper can be extraordinarily helpful.

On the other hand, I think writers—and many creative people—are more prone to despair than the general population, because one of the things good writers tend to have in common is that they're exquisitely sensitive to the world around them. That means they're more aware of beauty, but it also means they're more aware of pain. They live without much skin, walking around the world connecting to the world through nerve endings. This particular personality type makes artists more vulnerable.

TS   Earlier you made a beautiful comment that "despair cracks open our hearts." Can you help me understand this a little more, how despair cracks open the human heart?

MP   Pema Chödrön offers a wonderful teaching when she says, "The cure for the pain is the pain." We're socialized to avoid pain, to not feel pain, and instead to be perky. So we bury pain, we drink, we have road rage, we gamble or shop or watch a lot of television. One way or another, we are very good at numbing ourselves. The cure for that is despair. Despair is feeling pain and experiencing it. As hard as it is to experience despair, it's the beginning of revitalizing ourselves and re-experiencing our lives. It's the beginning of a growth project.

I had a friend who was diagnosed with a very severe case of throat cancer, and the doctor said to him, "You're about to embark on the most life-affirming project you've ever encountered." That's a beautiful thing to say, because people who get cancer realize how much they

43

love their family, how much they love being alive. It's ironic, but in my days as a therapist I saw many people stop feeling depressed when they got cancer. The despair it caused cracked open their hearts. Of course, you don't have to get cancer to feel despair, but you do have to despair, because for most of us it is the portal to waking up.

5

A Pain That's a Solution to a Deeper Pain

Robert Augustus Masters, PhD

> What our depression is "protecting" us from is
> precisely what we will need to face sooner or later;
> it is *not* something to be drugged, smothered,
> ignored, abstracted, or thrown into a dungeon,
> but something to unguardedly feel, something
> to cultivate intimacy with—and this begins with
> knowing our depression so well that we can reach
> *through* it.

Depression is not so much an emotion as it is a suppression of emotion, a literal pressing-down of emotion, manifesting as an energy-sapping flattening of feeling and self—but it is not a *full* suppression, regardless of its degree of numbness. As much as we may feel weighed down or burdened or crushed by depression, we nonetheless feel such pressing-down, unmistakably registering its discomfort and how it leaves us feeling drained, used up, enervated.

One could say that depression is the felt sense of not-quite-successful emotional repression. As much as our shutting-down flattens us emotionally, it still leaves us feeling wretched enough to darken even the brightest day. Depression, except at its mildest, is a kind of hell and at the same time is a "solution" to a deeper hell, keeping us significantly removed from having to openly feel and be with what is really hurting us.

If the pressing-down is massive enough—and such weightedness may be far from volitional—we will feel immobilized, sometimes debilitatingly so, pinned to the spot like a moth in a display case. Depression can be that deadening, our wings but petrified dust. The emotional suppression central to depression consumes an abundance of energy, running us down, but not so down that we don't feel anything. We don't just feel sad or hurt or lonely when we're depressed, but also burdened, squashed, heavy—as if the gravitational pull on us has intensified and our resistance to this pull is severely weakened. Thus do we sink, deflated and exhausted, slipping under the covers.

Depression is often explained away as "a chemical imbalance." There is, however, no conclusive evidence of this, though it may be that antidepressant medications themselves cause neurochemical disturbances in the brain, which ease short-term symptoms but create a health-worsening addiction to such pharmaceuticals in the long term. Unfortunately, most depression is looked at in the context of such biological reductionism, with far too little attention given to its possible originating factors. It is, of course, much easier to give those suffering from apparent depression some pharmaceutical aid than to actually help them explore—and not only cognitively—the roots of their depression.

We all get depressed from time to time; circumstances sometimes knock us hard, flattening us for a bit. We feel down, blue, unmotivated—but we are still able to function. We may skip a few workouts, complain more than usual, or feel unhappy, but we know our mood will shift before too long. This is everyday depression, a dark and rainy day when we'd like to crawl back into bed and stay there for a long while, but still manage to get the basics done.

Once we've developed some intimacy with depression, we may find that we even can, in a certain sense, enjoy our time in it, looking through its relatively unhappy, sobering eyes at the world and ourselves in a way that deepens us. At such times I like to write, go for a workout, or meditate. Sitting with depression can be fascinating: sensing the layers of it, the sadness and departure from positivity; feeling through it into our existential condition with an awareness of our mortality and fragility close at hand.

And there is a darker, more insidious depression, one that doesn't just knock us hard but flattens us with such force that we stay down, finding it so difficult to get up that we all but lose the will to do so. Such heavy-duty depressiveness may be situational—as when someone very close to us has unexpectedly died and our shock is so great that we cannot cry. And it may be already in our system, "wired" there from long-ago circumstances. This kind of depression requires strong intervention; unfortunately, this is often limited to medication, frequently accompanied by the assertion that we'll have to be on it for life. Medication is sometimes required, ideally serving as a kind of crutch while we develop other resources through psychotherapeutic, meditative, physical, and dietary means. Once there has been some healing and reassertion of will, to the point where we can stand with some strength, then we can start weaning ourselves from our crutches, being grateful that they were there when we needed them.

When we fall into a deeper-than-usual depression, but not one that's truly debilitating, it's helpful to ask investigative questions such as: What had to be depressed in our early years so that we could survive or cope? Why? What did we have to shut down then? What was happening that necessitated this? How was such a pressing-down or shutting-down activated?

Investigating the dynamics and originating factors of our depression doesn't require years of psychoanalysis or other cognicentric therapies; a few sessions with a psychotherapist who knows how to work deeply with emotions will in almost all cases illuminate the roots of what happened—and how that connects with what is happening *now*—pointing the way to dealing with the roots of our depression in a manner uniquely suited to us: ongoing psychotherapy, exercise programs, meditative practices, dietary balance, and so on. This takes a lot more time and investment of attention and energy than filling out a depression inventory for a psychiatrist, but it's actually far more cost-effective in the long run.

For example, when Kevin was young, he was shamed by his mother, who repeatedly told him he was stupid and worthless. She often told him she wished he'd never been born. Kevin's father did nothing, setting an example for his son that he should simply take whatever his mother said. No matter what Kevin did, his mother continued to shame him, making no effort to disguise her disgust for him. Kevin, of course, assumed all this was his own fault. He survived her belittlement by shutting down, literally depressing himself. This wasn't something Kevin did consciously; nevertheless, it became his default whenever he felt shamed by others or by himself (in the form of an inner-critic onslaught)—until he began working with a psychotherapist well versed in connecting past and present in more than just intellectual ways.

There can also be biological—but not genetic—reasons for depression. When Carrie was being born, she suffered serious oxygen deprivation, registering this as a life-or-death situation: pure physiological panic. To survive, Carrie's whole system had to slam on the brakes; her vital functions had to be depressed to conserve her energy for the emergency. This literally wired her to shift into a depressed state—so as to contain her agitation—whenever she was in a sufficiently stressful situation, especially ones that "took her breath away."

As such, depression is a pain that walls off—or keeps under wraps—a deeper pain. Such repression may initially work (it *does* actually distance us from our core pain), but it consumes so much life energy that before long we're depleted, run down, discouraged, further depressed. At best, depression helps us to lie low—and sometimes this is exactly what we need to do—but mostly it just exhausts us, as if we were back in the original circumstances that first necessitated it.

Depression is inherently draining. It keeps us under the bedcovers but gives us no real rest. A telling job description for it might be the "wretchedly insomniac gatekeeper of incarcerated pain or trauma." Depression's dreams are ones of hopelessness and meaninglessness. Our mindset during depression can easily reinforce our energetic flattening—we're in enough of a weakened state to sit passively before our inner critic's accusations, letting despair and thoughts of giving up occupy us.

Ordinary depression—which stops short of malignant despair or debilitating exhaustion—can provide us with a certain sense of security, a predictable and reliable weighting-down that generates an admittedly miserable yet also reassuring sensation of being anchored or settled, at least at some level. We may not be on truly solid ground, but at least we're not adrift in uncharted waters. Not surprisingly, we tend to prefer the burdened beasts of depression to the monsters of the deep.

But if we descend through the caves of our depression, entering what is walled off or buried, we find ourselves in the territory of our core or primal wounds. As scary as this is—and as important as it is to explore what's here consciously, caringly, and at the right pace—it is not depressing! The Minotaur (the mythic personification of our bottom-line fear) awaits us, its face none other than ours, our upcoming encounter with it readying us for a deeper wholeness. What our depression is "protecting" us from is precisely what we will need to face sooner or later; it is *not* something to be drugged, smothered, ignored, abstracted, or thrown into a dungeon, but something to unguardedly feel, something to cultivate intimacy with—and this begins with knowing our depression so well that we can reach *through* it.

Despite its flatness and capacity to dull our vitality, depression is an agitated state. If we are weakened enough, such agitation (usually presenting itself as a muffled, tightly corseted anxiety) may surface—easily running through us because we don't have the energy to push it back down—occupying our mind with dark thoughts and intentions, which only further depress us. Hence the importance of staying alert to the state of our mind when we're depressed, as we can through grounded meditative practices.

Depression is miserable in part because we can sense that it's a repression-centered state. It's very easy to indulge in. In a way, depression legitimizes our passivity; we can get away with grumbling about our discomfort and alienation from ourselves—without having to do anything about such states.

Depression is also a kind of numbness, lethargically and reluctantly facing its reflection in its stagnant waters. But when we look below the surface, we start to see and feel our core pain and unresolved wounds looking back at us. Then we begin to realize that in our depressiveness we've been treating such pain as an alien, a pathogen, something we are *allergic* to.

Depression, whether personal or collective, can easily slip into a toxic sulk, excessive passivity, or apathy. Depression says, "What can I do? It's no use," and its underlying agitation/hurt says, "I have to get out of here!" Quiet desperation and frenzied desperation, together reinforcing the trap. Or, depression can be used as a springboard into our depths, carrying us into the heartland of what really matters and becoming the doorway into what has generated it.

WORKING WITH DEPRESSION

The first step is to name it. Simply say, "Here's depression," to yourself a couple of times. Do your best to say it in as kind a tone as possible. Second, turn toward it. Face it. This is a movement through awareness, not through space—a shift from here to a deeper here.

Third, closely examine depression's various qualities: its texture, its density, its sense of color and shape, its directionality. Take your time with each of these, letting yourself be as curious as possible. Consider, for example, its directionality. This—its felt sense of movement—is very likely inward, a curling-into, a gravity-laden internal sinking, a withdrawal. You may think of yourself as down and out, but it is more accurate to say that you are "down and in." Keep your attention on this movement, noticing how it changes. Follow it without losing yourself in it.

Fourth, identify the sadness, hurt, and fear (and perhaps also shame and anger) in/under your depressiveness, taking time to feel and breathe into each. Finally, bring more attention to what underlies your depression—psychotherapeutic help is especially valuable here. As you do so, you will likely experience some very deep feelings, perhaps sensing yourself at a much earlier age. Approaching this can be a very vulnerable undertaking, so proceed only at a pace that allows you to remain present and relatively grounded.

Working with Depression

PRACTICE

Next time you feel depressed, sit down with it and bring your attention to your breathing, doing nothing to alter it or your posture. Instead of trying to get away from your depression, sense yourself moving a little closer to it, even as you remain aware of the arrival and departure of each breath. Do this for a few minutes, then shift most of your attention to your mind, noticing what is happening there, both with regard to content and energy. What are you telling yourself? What are you deciding about yourself? How seriously are you taking this? What is the general feeling of such thoughts? What is the felt quality of your mind?

Ask these questions at least two or three times, keeping some attention on your breathing as you make room for answers. Do none of this to get rid of or evade your depression. Have the sense that you are sitting in your living room with an unpleasant guest whom you need to get to know better, regardless of your discomfort. Stay with this for a few minutes, then slowly raise your sternum and deepen your breathing, as if to give your depression more room in which to stretch and move.

Stand up, plant your feet firmly, bend your knees slightly, and start letting your body shake, gently at first. Keep your feet in place, allowing yourself to move like a tree in a strong, but not too strong, wind. Shake out your hands and wrists harder, and now your shoulders, and now your knees and hips, still keeping your feet in place. Let your mouth open, allowing your face to shake. And your head and neck. Let your entire body shake, without any effort to do so smoothly or rhythmically. Shake as though no one is watching. (Doing this cuts through inertia, enlivening us and making more room for our emotions to surface.) Do this for two or three minutes, breathing deeply and letting your whole body loosen up. Then stop and stand still for at least a minute or two.

Open your eyes and prepare yourself for whatever aerobic exercise best suits you: jogging, walking, cycling, swimming,

> elliptical trainer, treadmill, and so on (this deepens and grounds our opening, getting our blood and endorphins really flowing). Begin exercising as soon as possible, continuing until you've worked up a significant sweat. Then rest comfortably for at least ten minutes, being aware of each breath arriving and departing, letting your entire body be suffused with your presence.

Depression is an energetic bog, a murky pit, a dark and despairing valley that invites our conscious entry, however indirectly. Descend into it, not resisting its gravity, feeling your way along its muddy footing through its undergrowth and dour mindset, wearing your awareness like a miner's headlamp, until you arrive at its heartland. Here, there is an abundance of pure feeling, and also a sense of encountering who you were before you were gripped by depression. Do your best to embrace and protect this you, this locus of pure vulnerability and unthinking openness, and learn to stand where depression is no longer depressing.

SADNESS AND DEPRESSION

If sadness were a color, it would be blue. Watery, cool, no yellow or red, just blue—and not a sky blue but a deep-water blue with indigo undercurrents. No wonder we talk of "having the blues" or "feeling blue." However dark its depths or its weight, sadness is not necessarily depression. Whereas sadness is the heart suffused with a sense of palpable loss, depression is the heart flattened so much that it cannot be felt.

Sadness is an emotion; depression is not. Although depression packs in plenty of feeling, it's more of a suppressive pressing-down of emotion. There is, of course, some overlap between sadness and depression, but they differ significantly. If we're sad and showing it, some people might interpret our state as depression, not seeing that our down-ness is a descent into the raw feeling of the loss of something significant to us rather than a squashing or pressing-down of us.

In sadness there is movement—down and in, down and out—but in depression there is almost no movement.

Where depression flattens us, sadness loosens us. In depression, we are immobilized; in sadness, we are flowing, however unpleasant that might be. While depression makes it difficult to take action, sadness provides a setting from which action emerges. Depression keeps us under the covers; sadness uncovers us. There's numbness in depression, but not in sadness. In depression we are drained, but in sadness we are cleansed. Depression is passive, sadness active. Where depression is repression, sadness is release. Where depression is mostly black, shutting out the very light for which it aches, sadness is merely blue. When we lift the lid off depression, getting out from under its heaviness, one of the first things we're likely to feel is sadness—not a moping or merely reactive sadness, but a sadness that breaks open our heart.

Working with Sadness

The first step in working with sadness is acknowledging its presence. Out loud, if possible.

The second step is observing what we're doing with our sadness. We might, for example, be trying to keep it quiet or putting ourselves down for being sad; we might be welcoming it; or we might be trying to cover it with a smile. Or we might be doing nothing in particular with it.

The third step is to make as much room for sadness as we can, assuming we're in a situation in which this isn't problematic. So we inhale more deeply, especially into our chest, moving our sternum forward and up. We're not trying to cry; we're simply making more room for our sadness to emerge.

The fourth step is to let our mouth open, jaw loosen, and throat soften, giving ourselves permission to release some sound—again assuming that we're in a place where this isn't problematic. Our deep tears flow best when the front of our body, from belly to face, is open, and our throat is part of this. So if the tears start, don't deny them vocalization; sometimes our sadness needs to be far from quiet!

Opening to Your Sadness

Recall the last time you cried, other than at a movie. Close your eyes, raise your inner eyebrows and forehead, turn down the corners of your mouth, lift your cheeks, and tighten your lips slightly. Breathe a little more deeply. Keep your hands in your lap. As you do all this, let your head come forward a bit. If you were to cry now, what would happen to your posture? Your chest? Your mouth? Stay with this for about a minute.

Now bring your hands to your face, covering your eyes, perhaps having the sense of cradling your face. Do you have the feeling that you could cry more fully in this position? Or less? How does it feel to "hide" your crying face? Stay with this for a minute or so, and then bring your hands back to your lap, lifting your head. Imagine gazing into the eyes of someone you feel especially close to, letting them see your full sadness. Let their compassion hold and support you. Now hold your sadness the very same way, caring for rather than shaming the sad you.

THE IMPORTANCE OF CRYING

Crying ought not to be something we outgrow. Deeply felt tears can be profoundly healing—at any age. When we weep, we open the heart, ease the belly, quiet the mind, soften the body. It is a loosening-up and deep cleansing, a washing-out not just of psychic debris but also—at least to some degree—of biochemical waste. The composition of emotional tears is different than that of tears that result from cutting onions or from an irritant in our eyes. Emotionally shed tears contain more toxins (much like sweat does)—thereby helping cleanse the body—but also contain leucine enkephalin, an opiate. So such tears both cleanse and ease us.

Crying keeps us from drying out. It is easy to slip into aridity, hardening ourselves against the painful or hurtful aspects of life. We may find a certain safety in such ossification, greening our deserts of abstraction with oases of distraction, but still sadness stirs in us. We can put a lid on it or keep it in our darkest recesses, but still it arises, calling for our attention, our care, our recognition. The more we suppress crying, the shallower our lives become.

The most painful part of crying is right before its onset. As soon as our tears are flowing and our throat is open, we hurt less, unless we're fighting and tightening up against our undammed tears. Even if waves of deeper hurt arrive once we've begun weeping—as when the details of a betrayal freshly seize us—the pain pulses through us with less obstruction than before our crying started. There is hurt, but it is the hurt of contracted tissues expanding and stretching from the pressure of what's seeking to flow through us; the more we resist it, the more it hurts. When we don't resist it, the sheer pain of it subsides fairly quickly.

> Each deep loss crucifies our attachment
> Our ribcage unable to hold all the ache
> It is not our heart that cracks
> But its ossified shield—its bulletproof glass
> A guardian from a much younger time
> Crumbling to less than dust
> As all constructions must

Allowing Old Sadness to Surface

PRACTICE

Generate a sad face. Breathe more deeply, close your eyes, and remember a time or times when you felt especially sad as a child. Let that memory fill you, examining it in as much detail as possible and feeling it with your whole body. If possible, place your body in the position it was in at that remembered time. Feel your body as if you were that age. Notice how your heart feels, your throat, your mouth, your tummy, your back. Is there anything you feel like saying? What might you say if it was entirely safe to do so? Keep your face in sad mode, eyes still closed, without any pressure to cry. If some tears come, fine, and if not, no problem!

Let your tears come, and not necessarily quietly. Let them flow, flood, storm, shake, and wake you. Let your whole body cry, weep, sob. Drop below any shame you might have about crying so openly, letting your heart break, knowing that what is breaking is not your heart but its energetic encasement. If you feel like a child or infant as you cry, let it be; keep your mind out of it. We have so much unattended hurt, so much muted sorrow, so much life force tied up in keeping our tears, new and old, from fully surfacing.

But surface they must, if we are to truly come alive.

6

Lifting the Armor
with Breathwork

Amy Weintraub

Practicing yoga is an act of embracing
all that arises with a developing sense of
compassion and self-awareness. As we pay
attention to sensation and breath, yoga
teaches us to respond rather than to react
to what is present. We begin to accept the
everyday stresses, the life-altering losses,
the unexpected betrayals without clinging
to the grievance or pushing away the
natural feelings that arise in response.

Through the 1980s, I wore depression like a suit of armor: armored against feeling, I was numb to joy and to pain, and constricted physically by its weight. You can't exercise in a suit of armor, much less practice yoga. I had meditated since receiving a mantra in 1970 and had even practiced yoga postures from books and records, but it wasn't until I took my first yoga class at Kripalu, a retreat center in Massachusetts, and learned to breathe deeply that I felt myself step out of the armor. Something shifted. After practicing a series of backbends with attention to sensation and breath, I dove forward with a deep exhalation into a standing, forward-bending pose called Yoga Mudra. In that moment, I knew viscerally in a way I could not yet articulate that the depressed me was not *all* of me.

There were moments in that first yoga class when, through my focus on sensation and breath, I had glimpses of my true nature through the fog of depression. Of course, I wanted more: I left with audio tapes to guide me through a home practice and returned to Kripalu often over the years.

Yoga didn't push away despair or tamp down the numbing fog that often rolled in as I stumbled out of bed. In the early stages of my practice, emotions flowed more, not less, as I slowly began to welcome and accept feelings that had been repressed. In those days, I often cried on my yoga mat, and the tears actually made me feel better. As my physical body was learning to let go of chronic tension through movement, breath, and sound, my emotional body was releasing too, without a story attached.

I still cry on occasion, and I love it when I do. My yoga practice is about clearing the space, releasing what blocks me from knowing who I am beneath the visiting mood or the story I am telling myself. Crying supports that release by stimulating the cranial nerves, which is one physiological reason we all feel better after a good cry.

Yoga is not just manipulations of body and breath. Nor is it simply a meditation technique that gives the ruminating mind a bone to chew on so that meditation is possible despite negative self-talk. Practicing yoga is an act of embracing all that arises with a developing sense of compassion and self-awareness. As we pay attention to sensation and breath, yoga teaches us to respond rather than to react to what is present. We begin to accept the everyday stresses, the life-altering losses, the unexpected betrayals without clinging to the grievance or pushing away the natural feelings that arise in response.

As the Buddha understood, our suffering makes us human. We can't escape it. But through our practice, we can create more space around whatever is arising. As we begin to understand that it is our clinging that inflames our suffering, we cling neither to moments of deep satisfaction nor to constricting pain.

We've all experienced times when we've replayed a scene or a worry over and over again in our minds, disturbing our digestion, our sleep, and our ability to concentrate. When we learn to clear our mental and emotional space every day with a simple practice, we still feel the barbs of life, but they don't stick. They pass through us without disturbing our equanimity.

In gratitude for my own journey through the darkness, I became passionate about sharing what had helped me begin to sense the me I was beyond my depression. I became a yoga teacher in 1992, collaborating with researchers and writing articles and then books to let people know how yoga practice had freed me.

Over the past twenty-five years, I've studied yoga with master teachers, followed and contributed to the growing body of research on yoga and mental health, and worked to keep practices simple and safe for students and clients. From the laboratory of my own body and my one-on-one work with students comes the most authentic knowledge of what works to manage depression. I've practiced daily and worked with people, closely monitoring the effects of breathing, *mudra,* mantra, meditations, and movements. I have adapted and modified traditional practices. Even the language I use to introduce and guide those practices has changed, based on their effectiveness to empower people to manage their moods.

Research has shown that the practice of postures, known in yoga as *asanas,* affects our biochemistry in ways that elevate and stabilize mood. At the same time, research has also shown that when we include breathing practices, the beneficial effect on depression is nearly doubled. Not everyone is willing or able to do a full mat practice, and there are countless yoga practices that elevate mood and do not require a strong physical practice.

While exercise is an important way to work with moods, and we can get that exercise from a vigorous yoga class, you may choose to practice many of the other timeless and evidence-based aspects of yoga—such as breathing practices—to clear the inner space and lift the mood. If you do choose to engage in an athletic style of yoga, then focus on your inhalation during class and practice some of the other healing aspects of yoga on your own. Or you may be able to find a class that provides it all—strong physical practice (if that's what you need) with a focus on *pranayama* breathing and tantric meditation techniques that anchor the mind with a *hasta mudra* (hand gesture), mantra, or visual image.

Here's a simple practice that helps us to meet our depression rather than deny its presence, and to begin to loosen its grip. It combines a pranayama breathing exercise with a mantra, a mudra, and a visual image (*bhavana*).

Bellows Breath (Bhastrika)

PRACTICE

First, let's create a little more space around the depressed mood or lethargy with a short, safe adaption of a yoga breathing practice called *bhastrika,* or "Bellows Breath." This breath is especially good for depression, as the experience includes mild elation, followed by a feeling of relaxation. During practice, the sympathetic nervous system is briefly stimulated. And following practice, the parasympathetic system is awakened. Blood pressure and heart rate usually drop to, or below, the resting rate, and the autonomic nervous system comes back into balance.

Please do not practice Bellows Breath if you have unmedicated high blood pressure. If you have low blood pressure, you might enjoy a little lightheadedness afterward, so be sure to practice in a seated position. If there is shoulder soreness or injury, practice Bellows Breath with the arms moving forward and back in front of the chest.

Various yoga traditions teach Bellows Breath differently. But in all traditions, both inhalation and exhalation are deep and forceful. I recommend that you inhale once per second and exhale once per second. If you increase the speed, you risk producing an overstimulating effect that can actually raise anxiety levels, and you might feel cranky and overheated. If you live with bipolar disorder 1 and have a propensity toward mania, too many stimulating practices like Bellows Breath can trigger a manic response.

Step 1 Sit comfortably with your spine erect. Bend your elbows and make fists with your hands, bringing the fists to your shoulders so that the knuckles face out, with the forearms and upper arms hugging the torso. Take a normal, natural breath in and out.

Step 2 As you inhale through the nostrils, with great force send your arms straight up, over your head, opening your palms to face outward and spreading your fingers wide.

Step 3 Exhale with great force through the nostrils as you bring your arms back to the starting position again, making fists with your hands.

Repeat these three steps at a moderate pace ten to twenty times, and then rest for thirty seconds. You may practice two more rounds of twenty each, pausing for twenty to thirty seconds between rounds.

Step 4 When you have completed the practice, sit for several moments, observing the effects. Feel the sensation in your face, arms, and palms.

Step 5 Draw your breath all the way up to the crown of your head with the phrase "I am." Exhale down to your sitting bones and say to yourself, "here." Do this two more times.

Do you feel a little lighter? Is there a sense that you have more room inside? Notice the spaciousness. Maybe there's an oceanic feeling or a sense of expansiveness. Enjoy that. Now from this place of expanded awareness, move to the next practice.

Imagery (Bhavana) *and Mantra*

Think of an image, or bhavana, that evokes a sense of calm strength in your heart and mind. This can be an image from nature, an animal, a face, or a time when you felt calm and strong. If an image doesn't readily appear, simply think the words "calm strength." In this practice, this image will accompany inhalation and, if it's comfortable for you to hold your breath, a brief breath retention.

You will be releasing the breath with the Sanskrit mantra *so ham,* which means "I am That." By repeating "so ham," you're saying that, on the deepest level, beneath all the obstructions—like the chronic tension in your physical body, or feelings such as fear and sadness in your emotional body, or the negative self-talk that might be going on in your mental body—there is no separation between you and the image for calm strength you are holding in your heart. Beneath the blocks and obstructions, you already are that. The seeds for your wellbeing are already planted. You just need to choose to water those seeds rather than the seeds of self-hatred and judgment that accompany depression.

You will be using a 4:4:6 breath. This means that you will inhale through the nostrils while counting to four, then pause and sustain the breath for four counts while visualizing your image, and finally exhale for six counts through the nostrils while saying the traditional (nonreligious) mantra "so ham." If holding the breath is uncomfortable, then keep it moving in and out through the nostrils as you visualize your image.

Step 1   Come into a comfortable seated position with your spine erect. Allow your eyes to close and begin noticing the breath as it moves in and out through the tip of your nostrils. No need to alter or change your breathing pattern. Just notice.

Step 2   Now bring your image for calm strength into your mind's heart. See that image or think the words. As you breathe in for four counts, extend your arms out in front of your solar plexus, the *manipura chakra,* which is your seat of identity and self-esteem.

Step 3   Pause and sustain the breath (or not) for four counts, visualizing your image for calm strength or thinking the words. Next, draw your hands to your solar plexus with the left palm folded on top of the right, as you chant the mantra "so ham." Repeat this three times.

Step 4   As you complete the fourth and last round, draw your image for calm strength into your heart. Hold it there with your eyes closed and observe changes in your posture, your breath, and your general wellbeing.

Do you notice a shift in your mood? Can you imagine practicing this again? Where might you do it and when? See yourself practicing in various settings—at home, at work, or any time you are feeling stressed.

Stair Step Breath (Anuloma and Viloma Krama)

PRACTICE

Here is a story of how one of my LifeForce Yoga practices, called Stair Step Breath, made a life-saving difference. Stephen is an intelligent, academically inclined adolescent boy who had been bullied by classmates for several years and had no friends. Stephen was not athletic, and often felt humiliated in gym class when he was the last to be chosen for a team sport. The ringleader of the bullies used the locker room as an opportunity to further shame Stephen for his slight stature and his mannerisms, which the bully identified as gay. Stephen had not experienced attraction to other boys, but the incessant taunts that followed him down the hallway and back into the classroom left him confused about his sexual orientation and deeply embarrassed in his school life.

Although his parents had intervened at the school on his behalf and the ringleader was no longer abusing him, Stephen's depressed mood continued to deepen. He developed one physical symptom after another, and his absences from school increased. He lost interest in his studies, and his grades declined. At home he was moody and often provoked fights with his younger sister, who was now accusing him of bullying her.

Stephen was introduced to the practice of Stair Step Breath, and after two weeks of regular practice, he was more energetic and started taking guitar lessons. The next week, he met a new friend who was into the same bands he liked. The friend was on the debating team and encouraged Stephen to join. Within a month, Stephen was working hard at school, had won a debate, and was talking on the phone with a girl on the debating team. By the end of the semester, his grades had improved. He and his friends were signing up for a yoga class the next semester instead of gym.

How could a simple breathing practice make such a difference in Stephen's life, and how might it help you? First, Stephen was given a means to control his breath. Research tells us that increasing feelings of self-efficacy creates feelings of empowerment and positively affects our moods. Second, Stephen was increasing his lung capacity with daily practice, and those little steps of breath, in and out, were stimulating his solar plexus, or manipura chakra—the area of identity and self-esteem. Third, he was letting the breath out slowly, which research has shown to activate the parasympathetic nervous system, which calms the stress response and sends soothing messages to the arousal system located in the limbic brain. Finally, Stephen was doing all this for himself. He had become the expert, able to regulate his mood.

The Stair Step Breath practice that Stephen applied is a mildly energizing breath that is safe for most people. The activity during the practice gives your busy mind something to do, so it is appropriate for both anxiety and depression.

Do not practice this if you have had recent abdominal or chest surgery. If you are pregnant, practice only on the inhalation.

Step 1   In a sitting or supine position, inhale through the nostrils in little sips—or steps—of breath from the bottom to the top of the lungs, as though climbing a mountain. It usually takes four to eight of these steps to fill your lungs.

Step 2   Pause and sustain your breath for four counts (at the top of the mountain). Imagine that you are looking out at something beautiful. If holding the breath is uncomfortable, breathe naturally through the nostrils.

Step 3   Exhale slowly for six counts.

Practice steps 1 to 3 twice.

Step 4   Inhale in a smooth, six-count breath.

Step 5   Hold this for four counts. Imagine something that makes your heart smile.

Step 6   Exhale through the nostrils in little puffs, as though stepping down a mountain. It usually takes six to ten breaths to empty your lungs.

Practice steps 4 to 6 twice.

Step 7   Next, inhale in little sips until the lungs are filled as described above, and pause for four counts with an image of beauty in your heart's mind.

Step 8   Exhale in little puffs as described above.

Practice this version of stepped breathing twice.

Step 9　End by inhaling in little sips, sustaining the breath for four counts, and slowly exhaling. You may wish to chant the mantra "so ham" ("I am That") on the exhalation.

Sit for a moment with the image of beauty you invoked. It's there on the altar of your heart, any time you need to remember that you are more than whatever mood is visiting.

CULTIVATING *KARUNA*, OR COMPASSION

When a difficult thought or feeling persists, we usually try to repress it or distract ourselves. Yoga encourages us to explore it more deeply. Research has now corroborated what the yogis understood: that spending time in the negative and then going to the opposite lessens the grip of the negative. We can use a yoga self-inquiry practice to embrace and then move beyond the negative mood state that is bringing us down. You might start with a yoga breathing exercise like one of the three that I've offered here, to open the constricted windows of your mind with a breath or a mantra or an image. When you feel a little more space, invite in feelings of compassion. It might be easiest to start with feeling compassion for a small child or an animal you have loved. Then bring that sense of compassion with you as you inquire about your visiting mood or mind state.

If this mood or mind state lived in your body, where would it be? Wait for an answer. Ask if it has a color. Ask if it has an image. Ask how old it is. It's obviously visiting you for a reason, so ask if it might be willing to share with you what that reason is. Ask if it has anything it needs to tell you. See if there is something you need to say back. Thank your visiting mood or mind state for being willing to share its story, and promise that you will come back to listen again when it needs to be heard.

Now go to the most far-fetched opposite of the mood state or thought that was bringing you down. It doesn't matter whether you believe it; just imagine it now. Breathe into that extreme opposite feeling or belief. If it lived in your body, where would it be? Wait for an answer. Ask if it has a color. Ask if it has an image. See that image and breathe into it. Enjoy this state for a moment. Imagine it.

Step back into the compassionate awareness that you cultivated as we began this practice, and see if—from this spacious place—there is a way to embrace both extremes. Is there a middle ground? Is there something between these two opposites that emerges in the form of a statement? Maybe something like, "I can live with things as they are," or "I accept life as it unfolds," or "I'm okay, just as I am." If it feels authentic, say it to yourself three times. You might want to write it down and then do some journaling around the process through which your compassionate self just guided you.

(

Our yoga practices can be brief and they may not even require a mat, but it's important that we do something every day to clear the space within so that we can fully access our feelings without getting stuck in them. Use your mat to weep upon, if you need to, and then roll it up and breathe into your day.

7

This Gracious, Existential Companion

Michael Bernard Beckwith

Seldom do we go deep enough into the paradox of depression and happiness to realize that they are not dual opposites, that they are a complementary energy flow within the indisputable polarity of human existence. Both are rich, skillful material to work with, flowing and overlapping like clouds passing through the sky of awareness, teaching us about the impermanence of emotions, feelings, states of mind, of all that is not part of our inherently enlightened self.

There was a time when for several years an energy of intense sadness with no identifiable cause was my constant companion. Each morning it had breakfast with me, sat with me during my morning meditation, walked by my side throughout the day's activities, and at night joined me in the sleep state. Then, suddenly, without even a hint, it was gone. I searched my very soul for it as though for a missing part of myself. After all, we had become intimate friends and companions on the path. It didn't take long before I realized that its absence was not a void, and that in its place was a spaciousness which made me available to hear the intuitive language of the heart. While words of this nature don't easily lend themselves to interpretation, for the inspired purpose of this book, I will make my best effort.

In the spiritual community I founded, the Agape International Spiritual Center, I have the sacred privilege of being entrusted by individuals with their heartaches, aspirations, struggles, and transformational breakthroughs as they navigate their respective spiritual paths. I have affectionately dubbed Agape "The Beloved Community," because it is a gathering place for people of diverse cultures and spiritual traditions, including New Thought, Buddhism, Judaism, Hinduism, Christianity, shamanism, Wicca, as well as nontheism. Throughout my twenty-seven years of intimate contact with countless of these sincere seekers, I have become aware of a shared common denominator: the desire for happiness and the avoidance of pain, especially in the form of depression.

When describing the textures of depression, individuals share how they are engulfed by intense meaninglessness, shame, guilt, anger, hopelessness, doubt, anxiety, confusion, a profound loss of a sense of self. While some pray for their depression to be taken away, such a prayer is so depressing in itself that it can conceivably depress the deity to whom they pray! Others try blaring out affirmations in an effort to deny or halt depression's intrusion, or double-up on the time spent on their meditation cushion hoping to transcend their anguish. Addictive behaviors, distractions, or over-the-top cheerfulness are other antidotes of choice. When the gauntlet of depression is thrown in the face of a prideful ego—as in, "I've been doing it soooo right! I have an enlightened guru and her profound teachings promise bliss, *not* depression!"—the ground of practice becomes painfully wobbly. Trust is supplanted by doubt.

In our "think positive—be happy" driven culture, individuals can feel pressured to be constantly "on," seldom waiting for temporary feelings of sadness or unhappiness to pass before swallowing an antidepressant. Pausing long enough to self-examine what may be the soul's longing for authenticity is not considered, so what is felt to be depression is oftentimes a disintegration that precedes a reintegration of one's true Self. Television advertisements sponsored by pharmaceutical companies showing the extreme contrast of the before-and-after impact of their antidepressants on a person makes such medications appear a highly desirable antidote, even when the list of side effects, which can include death, is read at breakneck speed.

Added to this are the fear and stigma that have been created in our society about a diagnosis of genuine clinical depression, a serious medical illness that negatively affects how a person feels, thinks, and acts. Data released by the US Centers for Disease Control and Prevention in January 2012 reported that 11 percent of Americans ages twelve and older use Prozac, Zoloft, Paxil, or other antidepressants. Let me be clear: Individuals who receive a diagnosis of clinical depression and for whom antidepressants will restore a healthy life—this is proactive. If medication supports a clinically depressed person in being able to initiate or maintain a spiritual practice, it is advantageous. My point is to emphasize that clinical depression, temporary unhappiness, and an experience of existential depression differ, as do their antidotes.

The purpose of this essay is to offer individuals experiencing existential depression—also referred to as the dark night of the soul—insights into how to welcome and relate with this Great Liberator.

THE ALCHEMY OF THE DARK NIGHT

The term *depression* comes from the Latin verb *deprimere,* which means "to bring down in spirits." We find a match for this description in the writings of mystics, including Kabir, Hafiz, Rumi, St. Teresa of Avila, and St. Francis of Assisi, to name a few. We read about Jesus the Christ spending forty excruciating days and nights in the desert, and how Gautama Buddha struggled with Mara the Tempter just before his enlightenment. It is recorded that Muhammad underwent the dark night of the soul that lasted for three years, a time during which he even considered suicide before receiving the revelation that brought illuminating light to his depressed spirit. Neither Jeremiah of biblical times nor Arjuna of the Bhagavad Gita were strangers to the dark night. By studying books about the lives of these victorious spiritual warriors and reading their writings, we come to deeply honor the example of their soul-artistry, crafted by surrender into the dark night.

During those times when I have faced existential depression in my own spiritual practice, I turned to the classic *Dark Night of the Soul,* written by St. John of the Cross, a sixteenth-century Roman Catholic theologian, mystic, and poet. It was through him that I learned the difference between psychological depression and existential depression. More specifically, I came to understand that existential depression is not due to external causes, that it is a profound *internal* expression of our unmet longing to realize our innate wholeness, our Buddha nature, our Christ nature. These encouraging words of St. John shine a numinous light on those times when there appears to be no spiritual succor within my inner reach: "O dark night, kindled in love with yearnings—oh happy chance! The endurance of this darkness is preparation for great light." Unifying with this promise, I find it easier to loosen ego's octopus grip of resistance and to surrender into the alchemical process of being transformed, rebirthed in the sacred womb of the dark night.

WHEN DEPRESSION DROPS IN FOR TEA

Can you begin feeling into the possibility of welcoming existential depression as a gracious, irreplaceable companion on your journey? The conversation might go something like this: "Ah, depression, thank you for dropping in for tea. Please, have a seat and make yourself comfortable. I'm open and receptive to the gifts of clarity and trans-formation that you have brought for me, so how shall we proceed?"

Seldom do we go deep enough into the paradox of depression and happiness to realize that they are not dual opposites, that they are a complementary energy flow within the indisputable polarity of human existence. To deny the paradoxical nature of our three-dimensional world is to fragment ourselves, to live from a limited perspective. Depression is how existence expresses to you in one moment; happiness is how it expresses in another. Both are rich, skillful material to work with, flowing and overlapping like clouds passing through the sky of awareness, teaching us about the impermanence of emotions, feelings, states of mind, of all that is not part of our inherently enlightened self.

ELEGANT STEPS IN THE DANCE

When we step onto depression's dance floor, we are not in the lead. So if our definition of fear is "not being in control," our dance steps will be ungraceful, inelegant. But when we are flexible, bending with the turns, stretching with lifts, surrendering to the drops, kicks, and swings, we are expressing our willingness to enter the mystery, even as we feel insecure and clumsy about the direction in which we are being led. Obviously, it takes the courage of a spiritual warrior, a bravery that propels us to continue moving forward while leaning into the sharp points, maneuvering the potential trips and falls. It's about letting go into the let-go, the willingness to free-fall, even without trust that the proverbial net will appear. It's about our surrender into unraveling the entanglements of ego, for as Jung points out, "The birth of the self is always a defeat for the ego."

The act of surrender happens through non-doing, another term for "effortless effort." It happens by being fully present for yourself and what is transpiring within you. When we drop our evasions we create spaciousness, and spaciousness allows us to be with what is flowing in our current of consciousness. The point is to realize that the light does not permanently remain, nor does the dark. Currents are always shifting, dancing, just as the day becomes the night and the night becomes the day. As a microcosm of the macrocosm, our innate nature reflects these energetic shifts as we participate in the dance of cosmic creation. The dark night is a gallant suitor. Seductively taking our hand, it asks, "May I have this dance?" A mindset of resistance responds, "No!" A consciousness of spaciousness responds, "Yes, indeed you may."

PRACTICES FOR NAVIGATING THE DARK NIGHT

My choice of the word *navigate* is intentional, because there's no practice for ridding oneself of the dark night. Once I dropped any and all illusions of being able to manipulate it, the dance was on. Eventually, with enough practice, I discovered three practices that convinced me *every moment of seeming self-disintegration is, in truth, a reintegration of the self with the Self.* I share one of them below, with the hope that it may be of benefit to you.

The Practice of Self-Inquiry

PRACTICE

This practice is an abbreviated version of the seven steps in the spiritual technology I created in 1986 and entitled the Life Visioning Process™, a method of deep self-inquiry yielding intuitively guided insights. I have tailored them into three steps specifically for navigating the dark night of the soul.

Step 1   Begin by finding a quiet, comfortable location where you can center yourself in whatever meditation technique or contemplative practice you are accustomed to. Don't overly concern yourself with the contents of your mind by passing judgment on what is arising and passing through your thoughts. You are the observer, the witness of the mind; you are neither the mind nor its contents. When you feel ready, move on to the next step.

Step 2   Begin your inner dialogue of spiritual inquiry by placing this question before your intuitive faculty of consciousness: "If this dark night never goes away, what quality must I cultivate to have peace of mind?" Rest in the question as you compassionately, patiently practice deep listening without forcing an answer.

It may be helpful to repeat the question more than once, or during another sitting session. Whatever the case, treat yourself tenderly; after all, you're bravely navigating your way through existential depression and coming into direct contact with your growing edge. Keep in mind that every individual's heart receives guidance in its own unique language, so you may choose to ask the same question in different words. Here's an example: "What is this dark night guiding me to release from my habitual life pattern in order to birth a heightened spiritual aliveness?"

Step 3   Feel in your very marrow a sense of gratitude for the opportunity to evolve in consciousness. It is not in the future; it is happening right in the midst of your seeming disintegration. What, exactly, is it that is disintegrating? It is the illusion about who and what you think you are, of the persona you've carefully crafted for public consumption and acceptance. Embrace the dark night with profound appreciation, saying, "Thank you for dispelling yet another one of my illusions." No matter how excruciating or messy the outer appearances may be, you are fully capable of simultaneously realizing how the dark night is responding to your stated claim of wanting to actualize the wholeness that you are.

Don't be surprised if at first you may feel hypocritical, as though you're fooling yourself into feeling gratitude, especially considering that there's nothing you want more than for the dark night to no longer hold you hostage. You are not a prisoner; you are being liberated from ego's machinations that would convince you that you are a separate self, that you are separate from the Whole.

ONE FINAL INSTRUCTION

When you walk through the door of the dark night, know that you do not enter alone. Remind yourself that you are being accompanied by all of the bodhisattvas, enlightened ones, and mystics who have gone before you. The dark night is a sacred initiation into a deeper realization and confidence that we are, all along the way, escorted through our lifetime by the presence of unconditional love, compassion, and guidance. And let us often bring into our awareness the truth that we are already equipped with everything we need to awaken to our innately enlightened state of being. Okay, one more final instruction, this being the second: celebrate your life!

8

Depression's Truth

Traleg Kyabgon Rinpoche IX

> Not noticing things is what leads us to solidify our
> experiences. When that solidification takes place,
> our minds become fixated on things and awareness
> is instantly dissipated. We are no longer in touch
> with our own mental state. When we are directly
> in touch with our mental state, we can see the
> changing hues of our depressive mood.

Depression is something we all experience. For some people depression is mild, while for others it is very intense and debilitating. For some people it lasts for a short time and then disappears, while for others it may persist over many years, or even an entire lifetime. We generally think of depression as a terrible state to be in: it is something we think we have to overcome, and we go to great lengths to hide it from others. This is probably because when we suffer from depression, our energy levels and motivation go down and we become withdrawn, uncommunicative, irritable, resentful, and basically very difficult to be with. There is also often a lot of anger, jealousy, or envy mixed with depression, because seeing someone who is happy only makes our depression worse. The point is that depression, in terms of its symptoms, can be debilitating and paralyzing because of what the Buddhists call the "conflicting emotions" associated with it. When we are depressed, our self-esteem and self-confidence plummet. We begin to doubt ourselves. We begin to think that we have become a failure at everything.

Western psychotherapists say that you can learn a person's reasons for experiencing depression if you look into their biographical or biological history. From the Buddhist point of view, though, the fundamental understanding is that depression is based on our interpretations of our life situations, our circumstances, our self-conceptions. We get depressed for not being the person we want to be. We get depressed when we think we have not been able to achieve the things that we want to achieve in life.

But depression is not necessarily a bad state to be in. When we are depressed, we may actually be able to see through the falsity and deceptive nature of the samsaric world. In other words, we should not think, "When I am depressed my mind is distorted and messed up, while when I am not depressed I am seeing everything clearly."

According to Buddhism, the world that we perceive—the world we interact with and live in—is insubstantial. Through the experience of depression and despair we can begin to see things more clearly rather than less clearly. It is said that we are normally charmed or bedazzled by the world, like a spell has been put on us by the allure of samsaric excitements and entertainment. When we get depressed, though, we begin to see through that—we are able to cut through the illusions of samsara. Depression, when we work with it, can be like a signal, something that puts a brake on our excesses and reminds us of the banality of the samsaric condition, so that we will not be duped into sliding back into the old habits again. It reminds us of the futility, insignificance, and non-substantiality of the samsaric condition.

That is extremely important, according to Buddhism, because if we are not convinced of the illusory nature of the samsaric condition, we will always be two minded: we will have one foot in the spiritual realm and the other in the samsaric realm, never being fully able to make that extra effort.

We are not talking, though, about chronic or clinical depression here, depression that has gotten way out of hand. We are talking about the kind of depression that makes us stop and think and re-evaluate our lives. This kind of depression can aid us in terms of our spiritual growth, because it makes us begin to question ourselves. For all these years we may have been thinking, "I'm this kind of person," "I'm that kind of person," "I'm a mother," "I'm an engineer," or whatever. Then suddenly that familiar world crumbles. The rug is pulled out from under our feet. We have to have experiences like that for our spiritual journey to be meaningful; otherwise we will not be convinced of the non-substantial nature of the samsaric world. Instead, we will take the world of everyday life to be real.

With a genuinely constructive form of depression, we become nakedly in touch with our emotions and feelings. We feel a need to make sense of everything, but in new ways. Now, making sense of everything from the samsaric point of view does not work. All the old beliefs, attitudes, and ways of dealing with things have not worked. One has to evaluate, say, and do things differently, experience things differently. That comes from using depression in a constructive fashion.

Depression can be used to curb our natural urges to lose control, to become distracted and outwardly directed, dispersing our energy in all directions. The feeling of depression always reminds us of ourselves; it stops us from becoming lost in our activities, in our experiences of this and that. A genuinely constructive form of depression keeps us vividly in touch with our feelings. In that sense, a modest form of depression is like a state of mental equilibrium.

Everything we experience is normally experienced from an egoistic or narcissistic point of view. But a constructive form of depression takes away the brashness, the security, and the illusory forms of self-confidence that we have. When we are depressed, instead of thinking with such confidence, "I know what is going on, I know where things are at," we are forced to be more observant and to question our assumptions, attitudes, and behavior. That is what we have to do if we are to make progress on the spiritual path.

The individual is then open to new ways of doing things, new and creative ways of thinking. As the Buddhist teachings say, we have to ride with life, we have to evolve. Life itself is a learning process, and we can only evolve and learn when we are open. We are open when we question things, and we only question things when we are aware of our inadequacies as much as of our abilities. Being aware of what we do not know is more important than being aware of what we do know: if we concentrate on what we do not know, we will always be inquisitive and want to learn. And we want to learn if there is that slight experience of depression, which in Tibetan is called *yid tang skyo pa,* and which has the connotation of being tired of all that is unreal, of all that is sham and illusory. The mood of depression can, in fact, propel us forward.

Even though many people who experience depression say that they feel stuck, the feeling of depression can be a motivating force. The Christian mystics used the expression "dark night of the soul," which means that you have to experience the darkness in order to go forward. You cannot just embark on the mystical journey and expect everything to be hunky-dory. You have to have the experience of the carpet being pulled out from under your feet and you have to experience yourself dangling and questioning, filled with doubts and uncertainties, not knowing what the hell is going on. As Lao Tzu says, "Those who say they know, don't know, and those who say they don't know, know." I suppose he is making a similar kind of point, in that the true, intuitive knowledge necessary on the spiritual path comes from doubt, uncertainty, and not knowing. The arrogance of knowing is expiated.

In other words, the spiritual path does not just consist of things that massage the ego or make the ego feel good and comfortable. The ego has to be continuously and repeatedly challenged in order for us to grow spiritually. One of the first things that the ego has to learn is that nothing in this world is stable or absolutely true.

In order to deal with depression effectively, we must cultivate five qualities in our meditation: courage, awareness, joy, love, and compassion. Cultivating courage means that we have to have the willingness to allow ourselves to be in a depressed state. If depression is the state that we find ourselves in, we should not become alarmed and regard it as a sign of something terrible. We have to have the courage not to recoil from our experience but to simply allow it to arise. It is not helpful to indulge in negative internal dialogues like, "How long is this depression going to last? Is it going to get worse? How am I going to be able to cope with myself? What will people think of me?" Approaching everything that we experience courageously will result in those experiences having no effect on us: on the contrary, we will become empowered by them.

This sort of courage is based on a fundamental conviction that we are capable of dealing with whatever it is that arises, rather than thinking that somehow or other what arises is going to have an adverse effect on us. When we start to think that our experience is going to affect us adversely, then fear, anxiety, and all of those things come up. But when we are able to say, "Whatever arises is okay," we do not have to be so self-protective. By allowing the depressive mood to be there—if that is what comes up—we are showing courage. If we have that kind of courage, we are not harmed. More damage is done by hiding behind our illusions and delusions; when we do that, the conflicting emotions become insidious.

Most damage takes place due to lack of courage. This lack of courage is almost like a pathological need to protect ourselves. We think, "I won't be able to handle this; it will be too much. I will be destroyed. I will go crazy." We indulge in all kinds of negative monologues. This is the reason our minds get disturbed, not because we have had such-and-such experience. It is not our experiences but our reactions to them that cause damage. We have to forget about our fear that we will somehow be harmed by our negative experiences. If we concentrate more on the courageous mental act of being able to accommodate and accept, we will provide room for the depressive state of mind to be there, and we will no longer react to it with alarm.

Having courage in meditation practice means that there automatically will be awareness present. Awareness means being able to see what is going on. If we do not show courage in our meditation, there will be no awareness either, because we will instinctively recoil from our meditative experiences. As soon as something disturbing or unpleasant arises, such as a depressive mood, we will recoil. We have to practice awareness in relation to things that we think of as harmful, as well as the things we regard as innocuous. Through showing courage, we can be aware of what we have allowed ourselves to experience.

Awareness is not a state, but a process: an "aware-ing." All of the mental states that arise in the mind are also processes. This is an important thing to notice. Even if you are in a depressed mood, you see that the mood changes—if you are aware. If you are not aware, there is no change, no transmutation, no movement. But if you are aware, you will notice that subtle permutations are continuously taking place: you will see that the experience of the depressed mood itself fluctuates. Normally we assume that it is the same depression, but it is never the same. It is always presenting itself differently.

This kind of attention is one of the things that Buddhism encourages us to exercise through the practice of meditation, because not noticing things is what leads us to solidify our experiences. When that solidification takes place, our minds become fixated on things and awareness is instantly dissipated. We are no longer in touch with our own mental state. When we are directly in touch with our mental state, we can see the changing hues of our depressive mood.

One sign of depression is a person's posture. In meditation, we pay attention to our posture. We do not sit with our shoulders slouched, looking defeated and forlorn. It is said that the shoulders should be extended and the chest out, showing some kind of majesty and royal bearing. That has to be included in the practice of awareness.

The way to stay in touch with our mental state is simply by paying attention to what we are experiencing in the moment. But when Buddhists talk about "being in the now," they often think that the "now" has no relevance to the past or the future. That is not true. The way to experience the present moment is not by ignoring the relationship between our present experience and where that experience has come from or where it might be going. The past and the present are embodied in the experiences that we have as human beings. Whatever experiences we have, we have them because of the past; we cannot have an experience that is totally disconnected from our past.

The reason why a particular experience arose in the first place is because of our past. That is the reality of karma. Our present mental state is the product of previous mental states and previous life experiences. In other words, what we are experiencing now is the fruit of what we have experienced in the past. When we pay attention to what we are experiencing now, through awareness, we are able to determine our future karma by making it take a different course. If we do not pay attention, our future karma will not be altered.

Besides courage and awareness, we need to cultivate joy in order to work with depression. Joy here does not mean elation, which is always a bad sign. When we are feeling really high, we crash really hard. In this context, joy means a sense of physical and mental wellbeing. That is, if we have good experiences in meditation, we do not feel too excited, and if we have bad experiences, we do not feel too down and hopeless. Joy in Tibetan is called *dga' ba;* it means not being like a yo-yo, basically. In either elation or depression, according to the Buddhist teachings, there is no real joy—we are just being swept along by our emotional currents. When we are happy, we are so happy—and we become completely overwhelmed by that—and when we are unhappy, the emotion is so strong that we cannot bear it.

Joy is more about being on an even keel. This does not mean that we cannot sometimes feel really uplifted and joyous. But if we have a joyful disposition—an underlying mental attitude of joy—then we do not completely break down when things do not go our way, or lose it to the other extreme when things go well. Instead, there is a sense of equilibrium. The fact is, we do not know what to expect: sometimes things will be wonderful, and other times things will be terrible. But having practiced meditation—having dealt with our depression and other states of mind—there can be that underlying sense of joy.

So dealing with our present situation is the most important thing, according to Buddhism. We should not always be thinking that things should be different, that something else should be happening based on our own wishes. If we stop doing that, we will experience joy.

Along with courage, awareness, and joy, we need love and compassion in order to work with our depression. In Buddhism, love and compassion are related to how we view ourselves and others. When we are depressed, we do not feel worthy of receiving love, let alone giving love. We do not feel worthy of receiving the gift of compassion from others, let alone capable of giving the gift of compassion. But through the practice of meditation on love and compassion—called "mind training" in Buddhism—we begin to realize that we have something to give and that we can give it. When that feeling returns, we feel more connected to other beings.

The gift of love or compassion is in the act of giving itself. We do not have to receive something in return to make these gifts worthwhile. The simple existence of others is what makes them worthwhile, because without others we would be solitary, lonely, cutoff, and miserable people. Life would be far less rich if other people were not part of our world. It is said in the teachings that even people who cause us difficulties help us to grow if we are able to deal with them properly.

Practicing love and compassion—along with courage, awareness, and joy—will keep what Winston Churchill referred to as his "black dog" at bay. That does not mean we will get rid of our depression overnight, but we do not have to. The negative effects of depression will gradually decrease, and our ability to make use of depression in a constructive fashion will increase.

If we are able to meditate and learn to develop courage, awareness, joy, love, and compassion, we will grow and depression will dissipate. We do not have to get rid of it—depression will get worn out by itself. That is important. Thinking of depression as an enemy and trying to conquer or overcome it, at least from the Buddhist point of view, is a self-defeating task. Our task in meditation is not to do that, but rather to learn the skills necessary to deal with whatever it is that we are experiencing.

9

"Welcome to the Human Race"

An Interview with Parker J. Palmer, PhD

This experience called "depression" is isolating to a greater extent than I imagined could be survivable, but I realize that this incredibly isolating experience ultimately reconnected me with the human community in a deeper, wider, and richer way.

Tami Simon   Parker, I want to start our conversation by talking about redefining the journey through depression and your experience of navigating through the darkness.

Parker J. Palmer   I like your emphasis on redefining depression for a couple reasons. As a person who's suffered three profound experiences of clinical depression—two of them in my forties and one in my mid-sixties—I'm aware of a couple of things. First, at the most basic level, our culture defines depression as something shameful. This angers me because it leads to a situation where millions of people are suffering not only from depression, but live in an aura of shame about it, as if it were evidence of some sort of personal weakness or character flaw. The good news is that recently there has been a more open discussion about depression, which is a sign that we're moving beyond the taboo state of affairs in which people who experience it are shamed.

Another way we need to redefine depression has to do with the way it has become "medicalized," which obscures the spiritual dimension of some forms of depression. I do not reject medical approaches, especially with respect to those elements of depression that are tied to genetic makeup and brain chemistry. I'm not against antidepressants categorically—in fact, I've personally been helped by them. In the short term, they put a floor under my emotional life so I could gain some clarity as to what was happening within me. My objection has more to do with the fact that many psychiatrists do not engage in talk therapy to help people make meaning of the experience, but simply prescribe drugs as the sole course of treatment. This tendency we have to want to reduce depression to a biological mechanism seems to me misguided and ultimately harmful.

So, redefining depression from something taboo to something that we should be exploring together in open and vulnerable ways; from something that's purely biological to something that has dimensions of spiritual and psychological mystery to it; and from something that's essentially meaningless to something that can be meaningful—all of this seems to me to be important.

TS   How were you able to make meaning from your three encounters with depression?

PJP   When I was *in* depression, making meaning was impossible—it was just an experience to be endured. For me, it's a mystery as to how people survive that deep darkness. I've come, over the years, to say that depression is not so much like being *lost* in the dark as it is like *becoming* the dark. In the depths of depression you have no capacity to step back out of the darkness, or move a bit away from it, and say, "Oh, look at what's happening to me. What's this all about?" When you *become* the dark rather than being lost in it, you don't have a self that is *other* than the darkness. Therefore, you can't get perspective and try to make meaning of it.

I often hear people say, "I don't understand why so-and-so committed suicide." Well, I understand why this happens, I think. Depression is absolutely exhausting when you're in the depths of it, and people who commit suicide often, to put it simply, need the rest. The mystery to *me* is why some people come through to the other side and not only survive it, but thrive in the wake of it. I've wondered about that question a lot, and I've never come to an answer that fully satisfies me. All I can say is that I somehow managed to get through the worst of the worst of times—and every time, it was a very lonely journey. In each case I had some help from the medical side, I had some help from the talk-therapy side, and I had some help from one or two understanding friends who knew how to be present to me in that experience.

Unfortunately, many friends and acquaintances didn't know how to be present to me. They were scared of me, I believe—they didn't want to come anywhere near me, as if I had a contagious disease. Or, they offered me well-intended but inadvertently hurtful advice that allowed them to leave their version of a "gift" in my hands—and then get out of the room as quickly as possible. Of course, in this situation, that doesn't feel like a gift at all, but a rejection, or even a kind of curse.

So when people say to me, "I have this friend or relative who's depressed—what should I do?" I usually respond, "Well, I can't prescribe in detail, but I can tell you this: do everything in your power to let them know that you're not afraid of them. Be present to them in a way that expresses faith and confidence that they have what it takes to make it through. Don't come to them with cheap encouragement of the sort some people tried on me: 'But, Parker, you're such a good guy! You've helped so many people, you've written such good books, you've given such good talks. Can't you fall back on all of that and pull yourself out of this hole?'"

When you hear something like that at a time in your life when you're feeling like a worm, when you've totally lost your sense of self, what you say to yourself is something like this: "I guess I've defrauded one more person. If they ever understood that I'm really *not* a good guy, and that all that stuff I've written and said is meaningless, of absolutely no utility now, they would reject me and cast me into the outer darkness."

Similarly, people came to me and said, "But, Parker, it's such a beautiful day outside! Why don't you go out and soak up some sunshine and smell the flowers." Well intentioned as it may be, this kind of counsel is ultimately more depressing than encouraging. I knew intellectually that it was a beautiful day, and I knew intellectually that those flowers smell perfumed and lovely to other people, but I didn't have an ounce of capacity in my own body to really experience that beauty or that loveliness. So the encouragement to get outdoors and see how lovely it is turned out to be a depressing reminder of my own incapacity.

Having worked my way through that very lonely journey—where only a few people were able to offer the kind of presence and support that I needed—as I came out to the other side, a couple of things happened that allowed me to start making meaning of the experience. One is that I found myself [to be] a more compassionate person. When you suffer, if you hold it in the right way, in a supple and open heart, you become much more empathetic toward the suffering of others.

Another way to say this is that you become less afraid of other people's suffering. You're more willing to be present to it in a faithful, abiding way because you're no longer treating it as a sort of contagious disease that you too might catch. You've been hollowed out by your own suffering, which makes space inside you for the suffering of other people. You're better able to offer an empathetic presence to them.

In this way, you start to develop a sense of community which, in an odd way, begins to normalize the problem. Empathy born of suffering says to you, "We're all in this together, and this is part of the human experience." Since having the experience of depression three times and emerging on the other side, it's very clear to me that the most important words I can say to someone who comes to me with almost any form of suffering—after I've listened to them deeply, after I've attended to them profoundly—are, *"Welcome to the human race!"*

No matter how horrendous their experience, there's nothing in me that wants to say, "I can't bear to hear this!" or "How could you ever let such a thing happen?" or "Now you've taken yourself to the margins of the human community." On the contrary, what I want to say is: "Welcome to the human race. Now you enter the company of those who have experienced some of the deepest things a human being can experience." So you start to make meaning of it, it seems to me, by realizing that this incredibly isolating experience called "depression"—and it's isolating to a greater extent than I imagined survivable—ultimately reconnects you with the human community in a deeper, wider, and richer way.

A second kind of meaning-making I'd name—after this opening into compassion that depression can help create—is that surviving depression can make you more courageous. After each of my depressions, I noticed that my capacity to put myself in challenging or intimidating situations had grown. For example, if I'm giving a lecture on what's wrong with medical education to a few thousand medical educators, that would have been a very intimidating experience for me thirty or forty years ago. I would have been operating out of a lot of fear and ego defensiveness. But once you've survived depression, you can say to yourself, "What could be more daunting than that? I survived depression, so the challenge in front of me right now doesn't seem all that fearsome." Then everyone benefits, because when I'm not threatened I'm more likely to speak from a soulful place, not an ego-defensive place—and my message is more likely to be well received, even if it is critical. So that's another way in which I think you make meaning: depression becomes a benchmark experience against which other things just don't look so bad. And since we have frequent experiences of facing into things that look pretty tough, that's a real asset, something of real meaning.

A final way that I've come to make meaning out of depression is through sharing the experience as openly as I know how to with others. But before doing this, it's important that a person's experience of depression, of becoming the darkness, be well integrated into his or her self-image and self-understanding. If there is any residue of shame or a sense of being personally flawed, then the experience may not be ready to be shared, and it could in fact be unhelpful or even dangerous to do so.

After my first depression, which was in my mid-forties, it took me ten years to feel that it was well integrated enough that I could begin to write and speak about it. Only then did I have the ability to say, "Yes, I am all of the above. I am my darkness and I am my light. I am a guy who spent months cowering in a corner with the shades pulled down, as well as a guy who can get on stage in front of several thousand physicians and deliver some challenging messages. I am all of that, and I don't need to hide any of it." It's my way of saying to myself, "Welcome to the human race! We humans are a very mixed bag—and, Parker, that includes you!" As soon as I was able honestly to say that to myself, I was ready to share my experience in ways that can be healing, therapeutic, and encouraging for others.

TS   For those whose experience is *being* the dark itself, and who are not in a place to make meaning of their depression, what do you say? I know you're not going to give any kind of trite feel-good answer, but what *can* you say to somebody in that state?

PJP   I'm not sure words can help in that situation. During my depression, the one friend who best understood what I was going through came to my house each afternoon. He sat me down in an easy chair, removed my shoes and socks, and massaged my feet for maybe half an hour. He hardly ever said anything. He was a man somewhat older than I, a very intuitive man, a Quaker to whom the silence came naturally. Somehow, by intuition, he found the one place in my body where I could feel connected with another human being. The simple, wordless act of massaging my feet was a lifeline that kept me at least somewhat connected with the human race in the midst of this incredibly isolating experience. He would occasionally say a few words, but they would be mirrorlike, reflective of his intuition of what was going on with me, never advising, never cheerleading, never requiring conversation. So he might say, "I feel your struggle today," and that would be it. Or he might say, "It feels like you're a little stronger today," and that would be it.

If someone is feeling they *are* the darkness rather than just being lost *in* the dark, it's hard for me to imagine that words would hold much meaning for them. Perhaps a glimmer of hope would come if the words were uttered by a person who's been in that place and can articulate what that place is like from a post-depression perspective. But I think the most important thing that a depressed person could do for themselves, if they have the energy to do it, is to seek out the kind of simple presence my Quaker friend gave to me. And offering that kind of presence is, of course, the most important thing friends and family can do for a loved one who's depressed.

It's also important, I think, for a depressed person to do something physical or bodily. I was barely able to go outside during my experiences of depression, in part because I didn't want to have social encounters. The idea of running across someone I knew and having a conversation was terrifying to me. But what I *could* do was to get on my bike and find some comfort in that kind of physical activity, zooming right by people who might want to talk. Walking would sometimes help, but only at night when no one else was around. I also found it helpful to keep a simple—and I mean *simple*—journal of small accomplishments: "Got out of bed at 10 a.m. today, half an hour earlier than yesterday." "Rode my bike for fifteen minutes, twice as long as I did yesterday." I came to value minor victories that way, and eventually could see an upward curve of returning health.

When you're in that deep, dark place, verbal encouragement doesn't work. We have all these images from our spiritual traditions about "the cloud of unknowing," or the deep and wordless darkness of the void before life begins. These are environments where there's not a lot of meaningless chitchat, to say the least! When you're depressed, most words sound like empty babble.

TS   Why do you think people are so afraid of depression and bringing it more out into the open?

PJP   I think it's because they don't want to risk further isolation or marginalization. In our culture, it's very common for people who are suffering to find that others [avoid] them. If you're going through a divorce, for example, there will be people who would have talked easily with you prior to the divorce, but who now, as they say, "just don't know what to say." Similarly, if a spouse or a child dies, or a tragedy of that proportion occurs in a family, we're afraid of it and "don't know what to say."

Now, it's interesting to reflect on why that is. I think we live in a culture where we regard everything as a problem that needs to be fixed. But we don't know how to fix things like those I just named, so we try to avoid people who have suffered that way. Key to opening up this emotional gridlock is to realize that we cannot "fix" each other, and shouldn't even try. If we can get that monkey off our backs, we will find ways to be fully present to one another.

There's an instructive parallel here to sitting at the bedside of a dying person. In this situation, we know that what we are looking at cannot be defined as a "problem" for which we have a "fix." People die, and no one can keep that from happening once it's in its final stages. So if we're sitting at the bedside of a dying person, we give up the illusion that we can somehow invade that person with our little toolkit in hand and offer advice, suggestions, or techniques that will fix everything up. We also learn that the most disrespectful thing we could do would be to avert our eyes from the dying person, to look away in disgust or in frustration. So we see that there is nothing we can do about the situation but, at the same time, that we cannot abandon one who at that point simply needs our faithful attentiveness.

So at the bedside of a dying person, we learn neither to *in*vade nor *e*vade what's going on, but simply to hold it in our attention. When we're able to be present to another person in that way, I believe we are communicating—without words—some kind of confidence that the person we're with has whatever it takes to make this part of the human journey in their own time, in their own way, and with their own inner resources. Looking back, I'm convinced that that's what the friend who massaged my feet communicated to me, that *he* had a certain confidence in me that I didn't have in myself. And because he was not afraid of me, I could slowly start being less afraid of myself.

As long as we relate to depressed people on the assumption that we have to fix them, then of course we're not going to know what to say, because there's no fix. But if we let go of that assumption, we can find ways to be present to them that are life giving, confidence inducing, and connective, helping them rebuild that bridge back to the human community. If we can show up without a fix in mind, the message is,

"Welcome to the human race." Otherwise, the message is, "I'm going to take you on as a project to make me feel good about myself." I can't think of anything more alienating to someone who's truly suffering than to be made into a project that allows other people to try to prove what skillful fixers they are.

TS   When you look back at your three passages through depression, could you say there was some intelligence at work? Was there something important that was needing to be worked out in you?

PJP   My general belief is that there is vast intelligence at work in all of life, embedded in life itself. It knows how to weave together the shadow and the light, life and death, and to hold that complex mix in a way the human mind cannot.

A lot of wisdom traditions have this notion that the little deaths in life—disappointment, failure, loss, etc.—can help prepare us for the big death if they are consciously embraced. From this perspective, it's possible to understand depression as one of the "little deaths" that life itself gives us, which are always chances to practice for the "big death" that all of us will experience. I think of that as part of the life's intelligence.

I don't mean that there's an intelligence that intentionally *made* me depressed. But I do think that an intelligence larger than my own accompanied me on the journey, giving me clues about how to practice a certain form of dying—one that's as close as I'm likely to come to dying before I die. For me, the process of surviving depression was laced with an intelligence that worked in and through me as I sifted and winnowed the experience and learned whatever I needed to learn from it, or at least whatever I could.

TS   When you became depressed in your sixties, did you think, "Oh, my God. I went through this in my forties, twice; I can't believe this is happening again. This is just terrible"?

PJP   Absolutely. I felt like, "Hey, wait a minute! This isn't fair! I've been there, done that. I checked this off my to-do list!" For me, my first and second depressions were in my forties, with the third depression coming seventeen years later. Seventeen years is a long time, and at some level I thought I was immune. It took me completely by surprise. But before I hit bottom, while I still had some cognitive capacity left, I was helped by the realization that I'd been in this place before, and somehow survived and thrived in the wake of it, so I might be able to do that again.

Still, as I found myself sinking and starting to recognize the signs, I was angry—at least when I still had the capacity to be angry. Ultimately, when you're in the depths of depression, you really have no emotional capacity at *all*. As I like to say to people who've never been there, clinical depression is not about feeling profoundly sad—it's about the terrifying realization that you can feel nothing at all. That's why the friend who came and rubbed my feet and evoked a little feeling in my body gave me a miraculous sense of connection, a small degree of recovery from this totally numbing experience.

According to the experts I've spoken with, there's a lot about depression that we just don't understand. So we need an appropriate humility, I think, when it comes to approaching one of the real mysteries of human life. By my rough reckoning, all three of my depressions were partly biological and partly situational. There is some history of depression in my family, going back through several generations, so it's not inconceivable that I have some genetic predisposition. But in each of my depressions I could also identify situational elements that contributed to it. When I was sixty-five, one of those elements was that I developed a growing awareness of my own aging and mortality, developed the then-depressing realization that I had a lot fewer years of life ahead of me than I had behind me.

I mean, sixty-five is a kind of symbolic marker on the road of life that says, "You're really getting old!" So as I emerged from that depression, I felt drawn to do some deep thinking, deep meditating, deep talking and writing—in my own journals at least—about death and dying. The experience compelled me to engage with my own mortality more honestly and profoundly, so that it wouldn't rear up and take me by surprise the way depression had.

And so, again, depression served as a befriending force in my life. And that prompts me to tell a story that comes from one of the depressions during my forties. In my second depression, I worked with a therapist who listened to me very carefully for a long period of time, over a number of meetings. I felt that this was somebody who was really hearing me, so when he spoke, I was ready to listen. At one critical meeting, he said to me, "You know, Parker, you seem to be imaging depression as the hand of an enemy trying to crush you. I wonder if it would be possible for you to image your depression as the *hand of a friend* trying to press you down to ground on which it's safe to stand?"

Those words didn't change things overnight, of course—but they made a real impression on me. I knew that something important had been said, something worth exploring and trying to understand more deeply. My therapist's comment helped me realize that I had been living at "altitude," and I managed to identify several ways in which that was the case. There was the altitude of living in my ego and my intellect, rather than in my body and soul. There was the altitude of having embraced a kind of spirituality that was more about up, up, and away than it was down to the ground of our being. And there was an altitude involved in a kind of "ethical ambition" that was all about flying high and emulating my heroes, rather than serving in ways that were within my reach, available to me.

When you live life at altitude and then trip and fall—which we all do every day—you have a long way to fall and you may kill yourself. But if you're standing on the ground, you can fall again and again and simply get up, dust yourself off, and take the next step.

That's the way I started to make sense of this notion that depression could be a befriending force "pressing you down to ground on which it's safe to stand." It's been interesting to me that over the last fifteen years or so, since I first wrote about it, many people have said that my analysis of altitude—and of the difference between living at altitude and living on the ground—spoke to their condition and helped them understand what was going on with *them*.

The depression I had in 2004, at age sixty-five, was also partly around the political situation in our country. I think we pick up depressive forces not only from our psyches, genetic makeup, and brain chemistry, but also from the social environment in which we live. In 2004, American political life, which I've always cared about, was a very depressing scene.

One thing I've learned is that once you get a little energy, and are able to get some perspective on what's driving your depression, it's important if you possibly can to become proactive in relation to whatever that may be. One way I have of becoming proactive is through writing. So in 2004, I started writing *Healing the Heart of Democracy*. I began with a prelude where I talk about my depression—which was in part personal and in part political—and how these two are related. I found great illumination in studying the life of Abraham Lincoln, who struggled with depression throughout his life, starting at a very young age. Here was this great figure in American history who was so depressed when he was nineteen or twenty that neighbors would take him in and keep watch over him for fear he'd take his life. Lincoln never totally overcame what they called "melancholy" in his time.

There's a great biblical phrase, "A man of sorrows, and acquainted with grief." Anyone who's ever seen one of the classic photographs of Lincoln—and that means almost everyone—will know immediately that that phrase is very descriptive of the face you see in those photographs. I think it was this capacity to hold both the light and the darkness within himself that made Lincoln the reconciling president we needed at the time of the Civil War.

Lincoln was the president who didn't try to demonize either side. He was firm, decisive, and a true leader, but he did not engage in the demonization and the blame game that is so toxic in American politics today. One reason for this is that he had long experience of saying to himself, "I am my darkness as well as my light. I am all of the above." He knew better than to assign all the darkness to one side of the war and all the light to the other. So he didn't have any trouble saying, "This union that we treasure is one of darkness and of light. What we have here is not a *perfect* union, but a nation that's always in search of wholeness," because that's the way he had to live his own life in order to survive and thrive.

I really can't think of another president from the long list of American presidents who could have done what Lincoln did as a reconciler during the Civil War. His capacity for reconciliation *externally* came from his lifelong practice of *inner* reconciliation. I'd be willing to bet that anyone you identify as a public reconciler of darkness and light is someone who has deep and long experience of that same kind of reconciliation inwardly. You just can't do it outwardly if you haven't been there inwardly.

TS   Parker, I always love talking with you. Quite honestly, you're one of my favorite people to have a conversation with!

PJP   [Chuckles] Well, same here, Tami. You ask such amazing questions, and I always feel so totally trusting with you. I never feel like I have to hold back on what I want to say.

TS   You are the welcome sign; you're a human welcome sign. Thank you so much.

10

Practices to Reconnect, Retrieve, Revivify

Ann Marie Chiasson, MD

The pain and depression were inextricably linked, one with the other, and I had to dive into the physical body, the emotional body, and the energy body to become pain free at all the layers. Once I caught a glimpse of the mystery, difficulty, and learning that depression was offering, this "illness" became my teacher.

I was born with a congenital malformation of one of my kidneys that went undiagnosed for most of my childhood and young adulthood. What ensued was a chronic-pain syndrome that had an on-again, off-again course. In medical school, this pain became more marked—I had to be functional for ninety-plus hours per week, so the effect of the chronic pain began to show in my life. I began an exploration with my family doctor and urologist to see if the underlying cause of this pain could be managed and treated. As I became frustrated by the possibility of a life with chronic pain, I became emotional and fatigued. At one point, my family doctor asked me if I was depressed, and if the chronic pain could be a manifestation of a depression.

I took a deep breath and blurted, "Of course, I'm depressed! But the depression is from the pain; the pain is not from the depression!" He did not mention this again, and we continued to work with discovering the underlying dynamic of my pain. Right at the end of my medical-school training, the cause was discovered—a chronic kidney infection that had actually caused the kidney to become nonfunctional. I began the journey of being adequately treated, and the pain began to resolve. A few years later, I had surgery for the problem kidney, and then went deeply into energy-medicine modalities for two years. I became pain free. There was no more depression as well. The pain and depression were inextricably linked, one with the other, and I had to dive into the physical body, the emotional body, and the energy body to become pain free at all the layers. Once I caught a glimpse of the mystery and difficulty and learning that was presented, this "illness" became my teacher.

A few years later, I reviewed my medical chart and read multiple letters back and forth between the urologist and my family physician discussing the source of my pain as directly from depression and not any "organic" or medical cause. Here it was again, a one-dimensional view of a complex issue that had been oversimplified and overlooked. Interestingly enough, the pain and secondary depression have been the springboard for my life's exploration, continued medical exploration, and much of my current practice. They have led me into my life's purpose in my professional life.

Depending on the paradigm that is being used for diagnosis and treatment, depression can be described and approached in multiple ways. I find that the conventional medical model of treatment, offering antidepressants and cognitive behavioral therapy, falls short for most patients I see. So here I will share the techniques I find very effective both for the symptoms of depression as well as for assisting with harvesting the gifts and growth that may be available from a depression. I will share techniques I have learned as well as practice from the paradigms of energy medicine, depth analytic work, and shamanism.

The flow of vitality and creativity in the body depends on how open the body is and how connected it is to, or in communication with, the larger energy field around it. The reservoir of life force, the body's chi, is housed in the lower-belly area. As we age, we lose this energy, and, as we get older, we have to gather energy every day to replenish this vital force. In addition, depression involves a deep disconnection with this flow of life. This can be for many reasons, including a shock or trauma, an illness, or even a disappointment. In the Mexican shamanic tradition, this is often called *asustado,* which roughly translates as "fright." In these cases, the energy body pulls up and away from the lower portion of the physical body. The resulting situation manifests in a depression. Whether I believe that someone's depression and symptoms are the result of asustado or not, I think that reconnecting or strengthening the connection at the lower *dan tien* and root chakra with the larger energy field is the crucial first step for lifting depression. Bringing the physical body back into alignment with the energy body results in alleviating the symptoms of depression, often very quickly. If the symptoms have been present for a long time, using grounding exercises for a more prolonged period of time may be needed to remedy the problem.

The second aspect for working with depression is to retrieve what is being called for through the depression. Once connected, we can begin the art of moving more energy through the body and clearing blocks. Emotion is energy in motion (e-motion), and experiences need to be fully experienced. A depression is often made manifest when one has not been able to let emotions and experiences move all the way through the body as energy. When we clear the energy blocks in the body, what we are doing is clearing old illness, old trauma, old feelings, and old experiences—old somatized energies. In other words, to retrieve the energy, libido, or creative life force that has been trapped, we have to clear up what has become crystallized or stuck. Once the energy begins to flow through the body again, the wisdom, images, or issues at hand can be retrieved for deep growth, healing, and creativity. Without this work, the depression is stagnant, so to speak. The mystery of what is being revealed for development at the deepest levels of the soul, psyche, and energy is thwarted. While one can recover from the depression spontaneously, using the depression as a marker for transformation assists the transformation itself.

Finally, the last piece I find important is the revivification or revitalization of the new life force that is coming forward. It is not the same as prior to the depression, although the changes may be subtle to an outside observer. The new life force that is now available has to be cultivated and refreshed, letting go of the old ideas of creativity to embrace what is anew. Like a young sapling, this life force must be gently nourished and cultivated. Using the energy practice delineated below will assist and lead you up, out of a depression, and into the next stage for which life is calling.

I call this process "reconnect, retrieve, and revitalize"— reconnecting the body, retrieving the soul parts and gifts from the depression, and finally revitalizing the life force into its new form.

TOE TAPPING

This Qigong exercise allows the energy flow to move up the legs into the hips and lower dan tien. It will facilitate the gathering of energy for renewed vitality as well as the strengthening of the connection of the root chakra into the physical body, bringing about deeper grounding for anyone who uses this practice. Toe tapping also helps balance the energy between the body and head, and increases the energy flow in the legs, allowing you to become connected to the larger energy field of the earth. From a Traditional Chinese Medicine point of view, toe tapping stimulates the spleen, liver, and stomach channels; these are the energy meridians that are responsible for overall energy flow, vitality, and blood flow.

Toe Tapping—Before You Start

Find a comfortable place on the floor, and then lie flat on your back with your legs a comfortable distance apart. (If you have back pain or problems, do this in bed or on a couch or other soft surface.) **Do not do this exercise if you have had a recent knee or hip replacement or if you are pregnant.** There are meridian points that can stimulate labor, so pregnant women should wait until after birth. For a recent knee or hip replacement, rub a handheld vibrating massager all over your feet and legs to simulate the toe tapping.

Toe Tapping

Allow your legs to be relaxed and falling open from the hips. Begin to rotate or roll your legs and feet toward each other from the hips, as if they were windshield wipers moving toward and away from each other, and tap the big toes together at the point where they naturally meet. Keep your legs straight. Make sure that you are rotating your legs from the hips, not just from the ankles. Begin to tap your big toes together quickly. Do this rapidly, using the momentum of the movement to assist you in the process. The faster you rotate, the easier the movement is. To assist with the movement, I suggest you play drumming or rhythmic music with a quick beat. Close your eyes if you can, and relax into this practice.

You may notice that the tapping is uncomfortable where the toes tap at first, yet this sensation goes away in less than a minute. You may also notice that your inner thighs burn; this burning will also go away in less than five minutes, and will decrease each time you do the practice.

Toe tapping will begin the process of reconnection. Practice this twice daily for five to ten minutes initially, until you feel that it is effortless. After about a month, you can increase your practice to fifteen minutes each morning.

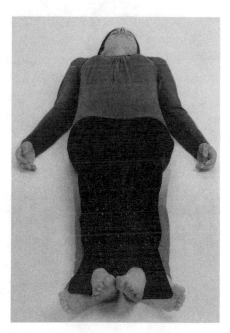

Figure 1: Rotate your legs inward and outward from the hips, letting momentum keep the movement going.

SHAKING THE BONES

This next practice will allow the depressed or stuck energy to begin to move. This also will strengthen the connection at the root chakra and continue to fill the lower dan tien with vital energy.

This practice is crucial for the retrieval aspect of working with depression; it moves the emotions and experiences through that are blocked, stuck, or residual in the body and the energy field. As it gives you access to experiences and emotions at the level of energy, you will become aware of different experiences, feelings, and realizations as you shake. You will be able to harvest the information and growth arising from this depression through image, feeling,

Figure 2: For Shaking the Bones, bounce up and down gently at your knees while vigorously shaking your arms and your body. The head hangs forward; let it roll slowly from side to side as your body moves.

and movement. I suggest you write down what you notice after you shake each day, to express what you have moved energetically in the practice after you use it over time. This movement is profound and powerful for breaking up the energy tags and blockages upon which the depression is based.

Shaking the Bones—Before You Start

Stand with your legs hip-width apart. You may play rhythmic music to assist with the movement. Avoid music with words to allow a clearer field for your own thoughts and feelings to come through. Anyone can do this practice; there are no contraindications.

Shaking the Bones

PRACTICE

Imagine a cord from the top of your head up into the sky. Imagine yourself as a rag doll hanging from this cord. Allow yourself to hang limp, with your arms and legs loose, and let your neck drop down, relaxed, in front of you. Begin to bounce up and down from the knees, allowing your entire body to shake. Shake the energy out your arms and legs. Allow your head to hang down in front as you do this. When any feeling, thought, or image arises through this movement, shake it out.

Do this for five to ten minutes a day at first. Once you get the hang of this, allow yourself to work up to fifteen minutes a day. Once a week, I suggest you use this as a prolonged practice: thirty minutes or longer. When you finish, take a few moments to notice how you feel. This is the best time to harvest and examine what is coming through the clearing, for your own personal growth. This is experiential wisdom; you must use the practices to open to the experience of the energy in the body being connected to a larger field. This will help stabilize and revitalize the life that is coming after the depression.

TAPPING THE BACK OF THE HEART AT THE ASSEMBLAGE POINT

The assemblage point in the Yaqui tradition is the point at which all the energy filaments from the energy field come into a person to become sensory data, which is then translated into understanding of human reality and cognition. In the Yaqui tradition, this assemblage point moves out of its correct place in illness, especially in a depression. Tapping on this point moves the assemblage point back into its proper place, thus effecting health and healing. In the Yaqui tradition, this is considered a form of soul retrieval—a method for revitalizing or reclaiming parts of the soul that were lost or were hiding in the unconscious due to trauma, illness, stage changes, or life circumstances. This point is also important in Traditional Chinese Medicine, as it includes important meridian points for health, as well as also being the location of the back of the heart chakra.

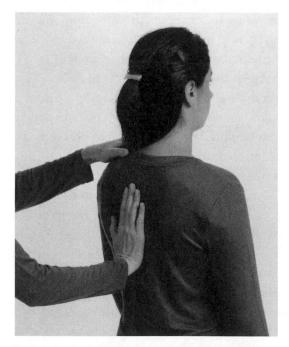

Figure 3: For Tapping the Back of the Heart, have your partner use his or her full, open hand to tap between your shoulder blades, the back of the heart center.

Tapping the Back of the Heart—Before You Start

This practice requires either another person to assist, or a handheld vibrating massager.

Tapping the Back of the Heart

PRACTICE

Using your full hand, tap on the back of the heart center of the person you are working on, at the assemblage point, between the shoulder blades—the same location where you'd tap to soothe an infant. Use firm pressure, as firm as is comfortable for the tappee. Tap here for two to five minutes, and then spend a minute tapping all over the rest of the back, starting at the top and tapping clear down to the top of the buttocks. Notice how you feel afterward, as well as any shift in your breath and chest expansion. If you are doing this alone, apply a handheld massager at the same location between the shoulder blades for two to five minutes, and then use it on the rest of the back for all points within reach.

HEART CENTER MEDITATION

The heart center, or fourth chakra, located in the mid-chest, is the most important energy center for healing. This meditation can shift the difficulties in depression, as the energy that is generated, amplified, and filtered by the heart center is intrinsically healing—for the mind and body. How we view the world affects how we perceive our experiences. When we view the world over and over through the same filter—often through the filter of "me and mine"—we can end up with repetitive thoughts and views that no longer serve our circumstance or life, and that can drain our vitality and energy field. Using the heart meditation can serve to give a larger view of the issues harvested through the depression and allow us to shift the way we see the world and how we experience it. The heart chakra is the great modulator: It allows us a glimpse of what is, not of what we want through preferences alone. And it is the unconditional love of the field that is able to see and accept each thing as it is. This is very important when someone is working with depression for personal growth.

Heart Center Meditation—Before You Start

The heart center meditation starts with the hands placed over the heart chakra, the right hand over the heart chakra and the left hand over the right hand. Allow the thumbs to touch. Look at the illustration of the hand position used in this meditation to connect with your heart center and augment the flow of energy. If you experience any difficulty maintaining the position as illustrated, try gently pressing your hands into your chest. In the beginning, you can also prop your elbows up with pillows. This hand position becomes effortless over time, so stay with it.

Figure 4: For the Heart Center Meditation, place your right hand over your heart area. Place your left hand over the right, thumbs touching. This hand position is a mudra, moving and balancing energy in the body during the meditation.

Find a comfortable, quiet place to sit. Keep the heart center attributes beside you to look at until you can recall all four without effort (see "Attributes of the Heart Center" below). If you like music, find a piece of music to play that suggests the heart center to you. I suggest you use the same piece of music each time you meditate; using a piece of music exclusively for this meditation will facilitate your practice. The music will become a gate or initiator to you for the meditation and the state of consciousness you wish to explore.

Attributes of the Heart Center

Compassion: Oceanic, limitless compassion.

Innate Harmony: Calm in the midst of chaos, the still point. Infinite, still bliss.

Healing Presence: Longing and desire toward healing. Love in action.

Unconditional Love: Unconditioned, unconditional love. Awe. Wow.

Heart Center Meditation

PRACTICE

Once you are seated with your hands over your heart chakra, close your eyes and begin the meditation. The heart center has four attributes—Compassion, Innate Harmony, Healing Presence, and Unconditional Love. Induct yourself into each of these attributes with breath and image. Once you have set all four attributes as the energy of the meditation, begin to meditate with your eyes closed. To continue to deepen, silently repeat one attribute with each breath. You may rotate through the four attributes, or focus on one attribute during different portions of the meditation. Set a timer (see below) so you do not have to track time while you are meditating. This is important.

Use this meditation daily for ten to twenty minutes. Use the Toe Tapping or Shaking the Bones first, before the meditation. If you open and clear the body first, the meditation will go much deeper.

QUICK ENERGY BOOSTS FOR DEPRESSION

These final practices will allow a quick shift or pick-me-up when you are experiencing symptoms of depression and do not have time to use the movements and meditation.

Ten Seconds to Center

This practice is a quick boost to both energy in the lower dan tien and the connection to the larger field at the heart and vitality center. Try this when you are experiencing symptoms of depression yet do not have enough time to use the movements, meditation, or any other of your tools.

Ten Seconds to Center

PRACTICE

Place one hand over your heart chakra and the other over the second chakra, below the belly button and above the pubic bone (see figure 5). Focus your attention and breath into the hand on the second chakra and on the fourth chakra. Focus back and forth between the two centers with touch and breath. Do this for ten to twenty breaths each time you use it.

High Heart Tapping

This energy center is useful for assisting the transformation of fear into service. Often the next stage of service to ourselves—life and humanity—arises from the development of having overcome a difficulty before. Our life's service usually comes directly from our own personal journey. While a depression can often be a launchpad for the next service into life and humanity, there is often extreme fear that we won't return from this journey. This fear can hold us back in the natural unfolding of personal growth and energy expansion. Tapping the high heart can assist in moving this fear into curiosity and action.

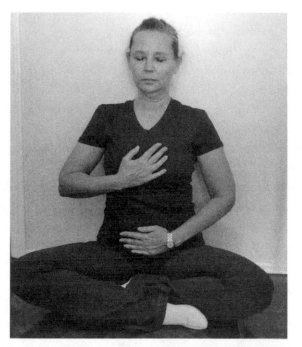

Figure 5: Place one hand over your heart chakra and the other over the second chakra. Focus back and forth between the two centers with touch and breath.

High Heart Tapping

Do this practice standing. The high heart chakra is located in the upper chest area. Begin tapping over the high heart. You can tap quite vigorously right at the high heart for at least a minute. Place your left hand on your solar plexus and your right hand on your high heart. Send energy from the left hand to the right hand. Next, flood both the solar plexus and the chest with compassion, gratitude, and reverence. When the energy begins to move, you may feel a sensation in your throat. If you don't feel an opening in the chest, you can go back and run more energy from the solar plexus up to the high heart. Continue to tap on the high heart until you feel expansiveness in your upper chest or you have tapped again for a few more minutes.

Use this for two minutes at least two to three times a day. Use it before the Heart Center Meditation.

Depression involves the life force, or creative drive, being dampened down. The energy flow of the body is not grounded properly downward, from the root and second chakra, down along the legs, to the field of the earth. The place where the life force, or creative drive, has gone is often described as the unconscious or collective unconscious. While this is a painful process, there are valuable tools here to be harvested. I use these tools in my daily practice. This journey does not need to be aborted or cut short, yet can be moved through quickly with the practices I have introduced to you. I encourage you to reconnect, to retrieve the wisdoms, images, energies, and lost parts of yourself that are in this field and that are normally accessible. Use these practices on an ongoing basis to revitalize yourself in the life that is offered to you after you've worked through the depression.

Figure 6: To tap on the high heart, make soft fists and tap on the upper chest, between your throat and heart center.

11

The Sadness in Bliss

Susan Piver

Maybe the difference between me and Chögyam
Trungpa Rinpoche, why sorrow feels awful to me
and, perhaps, was a source of joy for him, is that I
keep trying to close up my broken heart while he
succeeded in stabilizing his within the broken state.
Rather than trying to feel less, he allowed himself
to feel more. Somehow this is the road to liberation.

All my life, I have struggled with depression. I was born into this
struggle, and so it remains. Sometimes the depression feels like sweet
melancholy and sometimes like being punched in the chest. By Thor.
The feelings could last for an afternoon. They could last for a decade.
That's just how it is.

The other day I found myself in the supermarket, crying. One
minute I was squeezing plums and the next I was overtaken by despair.
I felt an enormous welling up and knew the tears would be unstop-
pable. Maybe I should have let the plum go and left the store, but at
this point in life I kind of don't care, so I sniffled and shopped. I paid
and walked out to my car. Once I shut my door, the wave of dark
despair escalated. I rested my forehead on the steering wheel and cried
and cried. Then I drove home.

I knew exactly what had led to these feelings. Earlier that day, I
had seen a photo of an elephant online who had moments before been
rescued from *fifty years* of abuse. Upon rescue, the caption read, the
elephant began to cry. The elephant cried. The photo of this great beast

was a lacerating image of the suffering we are capable of feeling and inflicting on each other. That in this case the victim was a gentle and intelligent animal made it absolutely unbearable. I shut my computer and jumped in my car, doing anything to get away. "Food," I said to myself, and decided: "I'll go grocery shopping." On the way to the store, I thought, *This is just one suffering elephant. There are countless others suffering in the same way, right now, this very second. And there is nothing I can do, right now.* I began to hyperventilate. I tried to push from my mind not just this suffering elephant but all suffering elephants, not to mention all suffering birds, fish, animals, and humans.

If you've ever tried to do this, you know it is impossible. Once the gate is opened, anything can come in. It is impossible to look away and also impossible to bear, which is an interesting combination. There is nowhere to hide. It suddenly occurred to me that every single thing I had ever done, created, purchased, or thought was in some way designed to put, well, *anything* between me and the awareness of suffering. Every book I read, every haircut I got, every shirt I put on, and every kiss I gave included the wish to not suffer.

But this is impossible. Now what?

It was Gloria Steinem who really began to help me with it all. The great feminist icon was being interviewed after the death of her husband. The interviewer asked if she was depressed. She wasn't, she said. She was sad. What was the difference, wondered the interviewer. Gloria said, "When you're depressed, nothing matters. When you're sad, everything matters."

With that message, she uploaded what to me is the most profound teaching on working with depression—to see it as masking sadness, that state of being in which the present meaning of things is clear. Yes, it is terrifying to allow the experience of rawness where everything touches you. You don't know if you will survive it, and it is possible you will not. I suppose that is why those who choose it are often called "warriors."

I'm delighted to announce that the alternative to the rawness of sadness—depression—may be worse. (Joking. Trying to lighten the mood. But it is.) With depression, everything grows faint. You feel remote from the people in your life. Sense perceptions are stale. You think the same thoughts over and over. Depression is deadening, claustrophobic, and solid. It is so still. With each inhale, you freeze. With each exhale, you fade away.

When you are sad, it is the opposite. Sadness is alive and full of movement. You feel others' sorrows in your own heart, and also their joys. Sight, sound, taste, smell, and touch become deeply nuanced. With each inhale, you feel. With each exhale, you offer. And you see the truth: All you have on this earth of any value is the willingness to open your heart. When you are open, you can love. You can make art. You can embrace being human. Interestingly, these things—love, art, and the wisdom of being human—have one thing in common: they are all things that arise naturally; they are received rather than manufactured. No matter how intent you are on, say, finding love, you can't go out and acquire it. Instead, when you create space for it, you see that it is already there. The same applies for creativity and truth, so to be fully alive it is important to know how to be sad. Chögyam Trungpa Rinpoche called this way of being "the genuine heart of sadness," and such a heart, he says, forms a foundation for the spiritual path that is trustworthier than belief or even study.

At first, I thought that the genuine heart of sadness meant I would be possessed by a sort of gentle wistfulness all the time. I would read the headlines and wipe a noble tear from my eye at the folly of humankind. Someone would cut me off in traffic, and instead of yelling, "Fuck you, asshole!!!" I would be filled with sorrow for the circumstances that brought them to such assholery. I would reflect on those who harmed me and, no matter how egregious the wounding was, forgive them on the spot and wish them well.

Right? Isn't that what the Great Ones would do? I thought about the beloved teachers from whom I have learned so much, most notably my own guru, Sakyong Mipham Rinpoche, and his father, Chögyam Trungpa Rinpoche—who introduced me to the Dharma altogether. I thought about Dilgo Khyentse Rinpoche. I thought about the Karmapas. I thought about Tulku Thondup and Mingyur Rinpoche and Traleg Rinpoche. I thought about Pema Chödrön. Would they be squeezing plums in the market one moment and sobbing in their cars the next?

Actually, I think the answer may be yes. It may be that it is not just the prettier emotions that count as the genuine heart of sadness, but also the wildly inappropriate and the mortifyingly uncontrolled.

I once asked Sakyong Mipham why it was that the more I practiced, the more I felt. The more I cried. The more I raged. (While crying. In front of two hundred people.) What was I doing wrong, I wondered. Surely the aim of all these practices can't be to run to your room and fling yourself on the bed, sobbing and confused.

He looked at me with tremendous kindness. I saw his own eyes well up, not with tears, but with love. He said, "You know, some of the world's greatest meditators have cried a lot." In that instant I got it that everybody cried, even the Great Ones. Even him. The Buddha himself may have cried with sorrow, frustration, and anger. When we allow the brilliance and confusion of this world to touch us, this is what happens.

Still, we have to get to the market. We have to get our kids to school, pay the bills, weed the garden, and make it to the bus on time. How can we weave such overwhelming sadness into our lives without tipping over into the kind of depression that freezes us in place and steals all of our energy?

Everything I have ever learned tells me there is only one way: *by feeling it.* Even when you'd really, really rather NOT.

Once I was in a meeting with a publisher to discuss a book I was writing (for which he had paid a tidy sum). He hated it. He hated me. We did not understand each other at all. I came to the meeting having thoughtfully considered his perspective, prepared to defend the points I was passionate about and compromise where possible. He came to the meeting with only two words for me: The first one was "fuck" and the second one was "you." "Fuck you" is what he said to me. Game over.

I was devastated, reeling, crushed. It was like inviting someone over to meet your newborn (in this case, my book) and having them pick her up out of the crib and throw her on the ground. I left the building sobbing, enraged, certain my life was over, with only my ever-diminishing bank account to keep me company. I hadn't taken ten steps out of the building when I bumped into my friend Michael.

Michael is a deeply practiced and wise practitioner in my Shambhala Buddhist lineage, someone I turn to unhesitatingly for advice and insight into the Dharma. He also used to work in publishing and would understand exactly what had just happened. He also didn't even live in New York City (where this all took place). That he happened to cross my path at that moment was absurdly lucky.

We sat down in a restaurant, and I said, "My meditation practice must be so weak if one person saying two words can knock me down so thoroughly."

He said, "So you think not getting upset is the sign of a strong practice?" I hoped it was. "It isn't," he said. "What matters is how directly and immediately you can bring your attention to what you feel. That is the sign of a strong practice."

Depending on the quality of the depression, sometimes I can actually do this.

Small depressions offer the perfect opportunities to try. These are the depressions that don't prevent you from living life as much as they color your experience in a darker shade. They may be situational, the result of not getting into the school of your choice, having an argument with a friend, or screwing up a job interview. Or maybe you're just kind of constitutionally morose. What helps is to simply turn toward your feeling and, yes, feel it. Allow it. Lean into it, as Pema Chödrön says, without—and this is the key to the whole thing—attaching a narrative story line to it. In other words, feel the feeling and let the story go. When the story wants to come back ("I feel this way because it is her fault," "I was raised by nincompoops," "I always attract the wrong person"), let it go and return attention to what you feel, which means what you feel in your body. Place your attention on the sensations (hot, cold, tight, diffuse, in the shoulders, belly, elsewhere) and feel into them, discern their qualities. Become very, very precise about your exploration. This seems to introduce the process of metabolization, a way for you to digest what you are experiencing and convert it to energy.

Medium-sized depressions are not addressed by simply creating room to feel them. That is only the beginning. These depressions could be for any reason or no reason at all. Maybe you were born with a depressive nature. Maybe you don't like yourself. Maybe you have inner issues that continually create obstacles for you, and you don't know how to change them. This is the kind of depression that is always hanging around; it lives alongside you. Feeling it is a good start but more is required—making a friendly relationship with it is necessary. Here, making friends doesn't mean having fun together. It doesn't even mean liking each other. It means creating space to hang out and to become curious about this strange friend. Our friends like it when we take a warm interest in them without an agenda (in fact, this could be the definition of *friendship:* warm interest without agenda); our depression likes this, too. We could actually become loving, open, and accommodating toward it and in just this way, develop some agency within our depression rather than being defeated by it. As we do so, we find that we are able to meet others in their depressions and, bit by bit, shift our attention away from ourselves and on to them. Far from making you a goody-goody in yoga pants, this makes you powerful—and feeling powerful is the opposite of feeling depressed. So, surprise, the secret antidote for depression is opening to it and watching it transform into a fount of kindness.

Large depressions also benefit from precision and openness, but something more seems to be needed yet again. These are the kinds of depressions that arise when a parent or child dies or when you learn that you or someone you love is terminally ill. Everything is permanently different, there is no way around it, and there never will be. Or, absent a clear cause, you could be in the midst of a lifelong depressive state that seems to have no beginning, middle, or end. Then what?

Well, I don't know, but I can tell you what I do when I find myself having fallen off the deep end. I remember something that dharma teacher Reggie Ray said to a student during a month-long meditation retreat in the Colorado Rockies. We had been practicing for about two weeks when a young man asked how long he would have to sit there before his agitated, frightening, dark thoughts went away. I mean, even after sitting for five or six hours a day they were unchanged, and he was starting to freak out. What should he do with his thoughts and feelings? Reggie said, "Well, you could always offer them to the deities.

They love the display." At that moment, this seemed like a totally reasonable suggestion, and we all nodded and went on with the retreat.

After I returned home, I reflected on this suggestion with the additional insight that I actually didn't know what it meant. However, that has not impinged on its helpful nature. In the intervening years, I've returned to this idea countless times. When I'm at my lowest and have no more ideas about what to do, I think, "Offer it," and something shifts. Even if only for a moment, I feel lighter. It's not a simple offloading into the ether; I intend my feelings as a devotional gift, a kind of mind-*prasad*. Even though I have no idea how my "gift" could be of any value, I offer it anyway . . . I know not to what or to whom. Maybe it's the universe. My teacher. Myself. Whatever deity I am meditating on currently, whether peaceful or wrathful. I feel a sense of gratitude that my depression could somehow be turned to grist and that someone or something out there is loving the mere display. I think of the bodhisattvas Avalokiteshvara and Manjushri and Vajrapani seeing, not my emotional puniness or lack of courage, but something now shimmery and now thunderous, now bright and now faint. Bursts of blue or red or green. Fireworks.

I have suggested this tack to students of my own. Most of them don't share an iconography with me so I ask them, who is your deity? I get all sorts of answers, from Jesus to the Great Mother to no one. No problem. Offer your depression to *that*. This is the direction of joy.

Once I was talking to a friend who was a close student of Chögyam Trungpa Rinpoche. He told me about a time when a student asked Trungpa, "What is bliss?"

"To you, it would probably feel like pain," he replied.

Maybe the difference between me and Chögyam Trungpa, why sorrow feels awful to me and, perhaps, was a source of joy for him, is that I keep trying to close up my broken heart while he succeeded in stabilizing his within the broken state. Rather than trying to feel less, he allowed himself to feel more. Somehow this is the road to liberation. Maybe this is why all the world's wisdom traditions tell us that the spiritual path is suffering. I don't think this means self-flagellation, but allowing the suffering that is all around to actually touch you.

Obviously, I am making all of this up. I know next to nothing about what went on in Chögyam Trungpa's heart and only slightly more about what is going on in my own. Still, the echo of this message keeps getting stronger the more I practice the Dharma:

Depression is what happens when I fight sadness.

Compassion is what happens when I don't.

Sadness is my engraved invitation to dine at the table of the Great Eastern Sun.

12

Into the Dark Light

Elizabeth Rabia Roberts, EdD

To descend, submit, and die—the openness to
being acted upon—is the very thing being asked for
when we come face-to-face with the transpersonal
for an extended period. It is a defining part of the
spiritual journey. The long periods of sadness, grief,
inactivity, and inner suffering that can accompany
these times are not evidence of mental illness
or a failure of emotional control. Rather, they are
part of a restorative and creative time in which we
have access to previously hidden realizations and
wisdom that can bring us into a new life.

It is likely, if you are past your mid-twenties, that you have had at least
a taste of the "dark night of the soul." You may have had months or
even years during which you lost your sense of purpose and confidence
about the direction of your life. There may have been feelings of deep
sadness and grief over what appeared to be lost. You were no longer
able to take any pleasure in life's offerings. During this time you were
overcome by existential questions: "Who am I?" "Why am I here?"
"What is life's meaning?" And despite your prayers, you remained lost
in a fog of unknowing.

This experience of inner anguish can be had at any age, and can
be triggered by many events: a debilitating illness, grief, sexual abuse,
getting old, ecological devastation, financial insecurity, traumatic accidents, the loss of a job or a relationship. In fact, any loss that strips

away the identity you have cultivated and become comfortable with can start a slide into a serious depression. The "dark times" or the "descent into darkness" are terms I use to describe this sacred journey that begins when one's personal identity is challenged to the very core. As painful as these dark times are, without them we cannot participate fully in the great rhythms of the earth. They are necessary for the renewal of life.

This journey can be initiated by, or accompanied by, any number of devastating mental and emotional states that can wreak havoc with our lives. I personally have been dragged through, or catapulted into, three profound descents into darkness. Each one was accompanied by intense feelings of isolation and meaninglessness. At those times when I was slogging through my own hell-realms, I felt no purpose, no direction, and no greater meaning. I was in absolute despair. These descents were so painful and lasted so long that they were diagnosed as serious depression—so serious as to be life threatening when suicide seemed to be the only option to escape such a living hell. While no one and no thing made these depressions "go away," I have been helped for short periods by medications, talk therapy, spiritual counseling, and energy healing. Sometimes I used several different modalities at the same time.

Each descent left its mark and resulted in a dramatic turn toward further growth in my life. But knowing this is small comfort to the one who has entered the darkness. The comfort of understanding only comes in retrospect. If I could have felt, even the slightest bit, a certainty that these desperate realms were preparing me for grace or growth, the pressure would have been relieved. There would have been hope. But the nature of depression is the absence of all meaning and hope—that is the essential ingredient of a psycho-spiritual descent.

Of course, not all inner suffering or feelings of sadness and loneliness indicate a tumble into the Dark. Patients ask doctors all the time, "Am I depressed?" or "Do I have a clinical depression?" as if the answer could be found by a definitive blood test, like screening for cancer. The only way to know if you have descended into the dark night of the soul is to listen to and watch yourself, to feel your feelings and learn to understand their meaning. If you feel bad without reason most of the time, you are in the dark night. If you feel bad with reason most of the time, you are probably also in the dark night. If you are disabled by your suffering, it is a serious descent. If your suffering is only mildly distracting, you are probably not in the dark night.

I have spent twenty-five years offering myself as guide and companion to those who are trying to navigate the rapids of a major life transformation. Through my roles as a rites-of-passage mentor, spiritual teacher, wilderness-quest guide, and trainer of other guides, I have sat in council with hundreds of women and men. One by one, they undertook their own rituals and came to tell their stories and pray for help in bearing their own time of "no answer." All I ever have to offer people through these threshold times is total empathy—no great wisdom, other than *I am here with you and I have been where you are. Take heart.* I feel with them, just as I feel with you. You are not alone. Someone is holding the consciousness of your greater world while you do your inner work.

IS DEPRESSION AN ILLNESS OR AN INVITATION TO ACCESS PERENNIAL WISDOM?

It is a tragedy, but not a surprise, to see how many adults and young people today are diagnosed with depression, anxiety, PTSD, bipolar disorder, lethargy, and other "mood disorders" or "mental illnesses." While these dark times are painful, it may be a mistake to universally label them as illnessness. Because as I will soon show you, religion, literature, history, and myth suggest they are likely to be a natural part of human development.

But despite our recognition of the frequency of depression and a body of historical literature suggesting the importance of dark times in our lives, Western culture seems determined to deny the inevitability of mental suffering. We are taught that happiness is a reliable measure of a life well lived. We are encouraged from childhood to jeer at loss, and told that periods of uncertainty, sadness, or extended fatigue are signs of weakness. Meanwhile, the realities of old age, dementia, and death are sad failures to be hidden from view. According to our culture, we are born to be happy, and to fail to do so is a failure to achieve the "American Dream."

It may be that our culture's greatest mistake, and most glaring hubris, is proclaiming to have found the answer to human suffering in consumerism. Consumerism is the belief that you and I would be happy if we only owned (or looked like) X, Y, and Z. Personal fulfillment now is defined by accumulating, not by learning to let go. We are told that we can possess our lives, our loves, our identities, and our belongings.

But we can't. Life is change. And the gap between this reality and the mistaken approach of trying to hold on to everything is the source of our pain and much of our depression. To experience extended depression and mental anguish in such a cultural setting brings a further sense of isolation.

We humans do not want things to change; it is one of the primary traits of human nature. But rather than showing us how to live in symbiosis with this unbending rule of the universe, our culture's primary strategy, developed over the last few centuries, has been to divorce us more and more from all cycles of change. Electric lighting, central heating, and air conditioning protect us from extremes of weather, from feeling the ebb and flow of natural climate changes. Large-scale farming, meatpacking, and big-box stores further insulate us from the constant struggle for life at the top of the food chain. And perhaps most devastating, passive large-screen entertainment and private pads have replaced direct contact with nature—and with the authentic storytelling and actual ceremony that might help us comprehend the overwhelming changes that surround us.

Despite what we are told, we all eventually stumble upon the dark times. And rather than presume we can avoid all pain, we would do better to encourage each other to understand how these dark times can serve as gateways to growth. As unpleasant as it is, suffering is the very means of renewal, discovery, and growth. Darkness and Light are both necessary for the renewal of life and the emergence of human consciousness. After all, winter is not a failed summer! It is a natural part of the cyclical round of Earth.

THE PAINFUL SEARCH FOR HAPPINESS

One of the most astonishing features of human life today is that we believe it is possible to minimize and even eliminate suffering—the inner pain of life—which is one reason why it is so difficult for us to even acknowledge that we are suffering. This is still the land of Dale Carnegie and Norman Vincent Peale, where an unflagging optimism is taken as the means and measure of success. We must therefore carry an added burden: *We feel bad about feeling bad.* We think, "This shouldn't be this way" or "I am going to get rid of this somehow." Some of us believe that since suffering is so bad, so hard, so painful, if we were really good and really smart, it wouldn't arise in the first place. Somehow the pain of depression, loss, anxiety, or grief is our own fault. If not, then it's definitely someone else's fault. In any case, we should surely be able to avoid it. We should set it to one side and not dwell on it. We should "move on," go on to positive things, do a little meditation or yoga to get around the suffering and go forward. We constantly go back to this way of thinking.

But depression cannot be banished by injections of optimism or sermons on "positive thinking." Like grief, it must be acknowledged and worked through. This means it must be named and validated as a normal human response to the situation we find ourselves in. Faced and experienced, its power can be used, as the frozen defenses of the psyche thaw and new energies are released.

As Pierre Teilhard de Chardin says, "Suffering is the condition for growing; everything that grows, suffers."

ANCESTRAL APPROACHES TO DEPRESSION

There is a lineage of both religious and secular literature reminding us that times of total darkness are a natural part of the human condition. These dark periods of inner suffering were identified as sacrificial moments by Christians, and Fana, or annihilation, by Sufis. The early Sumerians referred to these states as the descent to the goddess, Hindus referred to them as kundalini rising, and Greeks identified these initiations with journeys to a netherworld.

These times were recognized as important and transformational because suffering is the predominant feeling of the process through which a human being must pass as the ego deconstructs and the transpersonal self is birthed. Suffering and depression, precisely because they threaten and attack the defenses of the separate self, become the crucible of transformation.

Our ancestors identified these times of great confusion and inaction as "initiatory" states. An initiate is one who accepts the dark times on its terms. We may not like it, but we do our best to turn our most vulnerable selves toward the hottest part of the fire and wait patiently for the messages of the dark light. Most people begin to inquire more deeply into their lives not because there is joy, but because there is pain. Pain denotes the limit of the territory of the imagined self, the "safe ground" of the self-image, beyond which a kind of queasiness arises at being in the midst of the uncontrollable. This is our edge, our resistance to life, and the place where the heart closes in self-protection. When you are near your edge you are near truth—and that truth is usually defended by psychological and physiological demons warning that if you continue and cross over this edge, loss and death are on your path. W. B. Yeats puts it this way: "The price of a soul is sorrow."

To descend, submit, and die—the openness to *being acted upon*—is the feminine essence of the human experience. It is the very thing that is being asked of us when we come face-to-face with the transpersonal, and it is a defining part of the spiritual journey. If these dark times are a natural part of our spiritual growth, then the long periods of sadness, grief, inactivity, and inner suffering that can accompany them are not evidence of weakness or a failure of emotional control, as we are too often told. Rather, they are part of a restorative and creative time in which we have access to previously hidden realizations and wisdom that can bring us into a new life.

There is a striking passage in the Gospel of St. John in which Jesus says, "Except a corn of wheat fall into the ground and die, it abides alone, but if it dies it brings forth much fruit." In this context, the idea of suffering and death is linked with that of rebirth and fulfillment. In joining suffering and death with the idea of transformation and the continuity of a total process, life's apparent contradictions are resolved. Life does not die, but is expressed in constant transformation and movement. Ironically, it is this necessity of constant change that can bring the human mind into chaotic, irrational, and disturbingly helpless states.

SEEING WITH THE DARK LIGHT

Throughout history, cultures have given us many myths and stories that offer insights about navigating these "dark nights of the soul." The word *darkness* implies that we can't see with our usual sight. We are plunged into an abyss, a deep well of mystery, of not knowing, where we no longer see things from the outside as witness. Instead, we depend on the grace of an inner "dark light," gifts of cellular insight left by those who have gone before us. These glimmerings help reveal the underlying patterns that characterize every transformative journey. It is this other way of "seeing, that is not-seeing" that, for me, held the promise of renewal and spring.

A singular aspect of this process is the need to move from our thinking capacities to our deeper knowing, the light within the dark—those insights laid down in the right brain long before the gifts of the left, rational side were even recognizable. To make this shift to the powers of the earlier, right hemisphere of the brain with its liminal capacities for wholeness, image, raw feelings, and the transformational paradox of birth and death, the ancestors learned to help each other through ceremony, ritual, myths, and music. They seem to have accepted, more than we, that the dark times are a necessary part of life's cycle.

Over time, they created stories about a descent during which our old identity is stripped away as we await our rebirth into greater awareness and wisdom—wisdom that will serve not only the individual, but also the community as a whole.

A MORE PRIMORDIAL CULTURAL UNDERSTANDING

If experiences of depression, grief, anxiety, mental suffering, isolation, and other examples of the dark night are not to be relegated to a catchall bin of mental illnesses, and cannot be assuaged by a lifestyle of consumerism, how then are we to psychologically, culturally, and spiritually engage with life's deep suffering?

As tribal peoples have always known, when one person changes, it brings the challenge of change to everyone. When, after an arduous process, a woman gives birth, her status in the tribe or kin group changes, as does the role of her mother and her sisters. When a teenage boy returns to his tribe from his vision quest, which may have lasted anywhere from a few weeks to a year's solo journey into the wild, he is recognized as a man. It is understood that he brings new gifts to his people. His father and mother and others in his family circle all are called to change in response to these new insights and wisdom.

This is how communities have grown and changed throughout history: as one changes and grows, the greater whole is affected. Thus the dark times are endured both for the sake of the individual's growth and for the health of the larger whole. Despite what they are feeling in the moment, there are psycho-spiritual gifts for themselves and their people in completing the process.

From decades of working with myself and others who are going through a rugged life passage, there is an alternative, or at least a helpful supplement, to the medical regime we now prefer. Most people suffering through a descent can be helped by empathetic relationships and by understanding that what is happening to them is a difficult but normal human experience. They may be experiencing a descent and return experience that is as old as our species.

A STORY OF SACRED DESCENT INTO THE DARK

The oldest known myth that states this motif of a descent into the dark feminine was written on clay tablets in the third millennium BC as the Descent of Inanna (though it is probably much older, reaching into preliterate times). It can be seen throughout history influencing the far more recent stories of descents into hell made by male divinities of which the Christ story of the stations of the cross, denunciation in the temple, flagellation, crucifixion, entombment, and ascension is the most well known. Here is the story:

Inanna, queen of heaven and earth, goes into the underworld of her own will—possibly to visit her sister, Ereshkigal, queen of the underworld, who is mourning the death of her husband and is suffering her own birth pangs in the netherworld: "She set her heart from highest heaven on earth's deepest ground. Abandoned heaven, abandoned earth—to the Netherworld." This is an important difference from more recent myths taking root after the ascendance of the patriarchy, in which female divinities were usually "cast into hades." Inanna chooses her own journey.

As a precaution, Inanna instructs Ninshubur, her trusted female executive, to appeal to the father gods for help in securing her release if she does not return within three days. At the first gate, Inanna is stopped. She asks for admission to the "land of no return" to witness the funeral of Gugalanna, husband of Ereshkigal. She knows from the demeanor of the Guardian of the gate, a wrathful deity, that suffering lies ahead of her. True to form, Ereshkigal becomes furious and insists that the upper-world goddess be treated according to the laws and rites for anyone entering her kingdom—that she be "brought naked and bowed low," the same way the Sumerians are buried.

The orders are followed, and at each of the seven gates of Ereshkigal's lapis lazuli house, the gatekeeper removes one piece of Inanna's magnificent regalia until she is stripped of all signs of authority or honor. The procession to deeper consciousness requires the total sacrifice of identity—the upper-world aspects of the self are exchanged for the sake of the dark, repressed, undifferentiated ground of being. Thus Inanna is brought naked and bowed low.

Here one might expect a reprieve for Inanna; having surrendered all her powers, all her ways of being, we might expect that she be granted Ereshkigal's permission to enter the underworld. But the archaic, irrational potency of the descended feminine is neither nice nor predictable. It is the Destructive-Transformative side of the cosmic will. Ereshkigal, in her destructive fury, flings Inanna onto a stake like a piece of meat and lets her hang there dead and rotting, green with maggots. The myth conveys the complete horror of this underworld death.

The stasis of Inanna at this point seems to suggest dissolution and slowness, both of which require great patience of those who enter. Once in the dark realm, we are barely conscious. We are reduced to a slow decaying of all the "shoulds"—we are in the dark, amoral side of intuition. Here there is both inertia and an elemental healing source unknowable in the upper world.

After three days, when Inanna fails to return, her assistant, Ninshubur, sets in motion Inanna's instructions to rouse the people and the gods with "dirge drum and lamenting." Ninshubur goes to the high gods of sky and earth; to the moon god, Inanna's brother; and the sun god, her father. All refuse to meddle in the demanding ways of the underworld. Finally, Enki, the god of waters and wisdom, hears the plea and creates two of the most endearing creatures in all of Western mythology. Enki creates from the dirt, from the humus under his fingernail, two tiny, genderless mourners. They slip unnoticed into the netherworld, carrying the food and water of life with which Enki provided them. But first they align themselves with Ereshkagil, who is both groaning over the death of her husband and voicing her primal birth pangs.

They go alongside and commiserate with her. They groan with her, "Oh, my pain, my great misery," "Oh, your pain, your great misery, queen of the underworld." They offer no solutions or succor to Ereshkagil. They do not tell her how to get out of hell. They simply offer their empathy. Ereshkigal is so grateful for the compassion that, at their request, she finally hands over Inanna's rotten corpse.

Restored to life, Inanna begins her return journey through the seven gates, reclaiming each of her vestments. Ereshkigal sends a wrathful reminder to Inanna that she will need to send a substitute to take her place. The last part of the myth involves Inanna's search for her substitute, and the revenge she wreaks when Dumuzi, her consort, ignores her and sits enjoying himself on her throne. This last part goes on in considerable detail while Inanna is remaking her relations with all of heaven and earth. This is a reminder that remaking the Self takes time and is embodied in our reinspired life and its newly defined relationships.

The poem ends with the words: "Inanna placed Dumuzi in the hands of the eternal dark. Holy Ereshkigal! Sweet is your praise."

EMBRACING THE FORGOTTEN FEMININE

To me, Inanna is the most meaningful image we have of the feminine when it is approaching the dark night. The poem suggests that if we follow Inanna into those depths, we are given a sense of the one cosmic power; there we are moved and taught through the intensity of our feelings. There, the conscious ego is overwhelmed by passion and numinous images. Shaken, perhaps even destroyed, we are coalesced into a new pattern with a new power to reorder our world.

For the goddesses and gods of antiquity, the descent was never a story of confronting a little bit of darkness inside themselves; of dipping their feet in their feelings, paddling in the pond of their emotions and trying to bring them into the light of day. It was a question of going right through that darkness to what lies at the other end. It was always a death experience.

Over time, these myths were amputated. Western philosophy learned to focus on the One, the True, the Good and the Beautiful, and cut out the need for the descent. This permitted cerebral-intellectual Apollonian, left-brain consciousness, with its ethical and conceptual discriminations, to become dominant. We no longer even notice that it happened. The problem is that when the divine is removed from the depths, particularly the feminine depths, we weaken our own interiority and start viewing the depths with fear. We end up struggling, running from ourselves, trying to lift ourselves up by our bootstraps into the beyond. But it is impossible to reach the light at the cost of rejecting the darkness.

The darkness haunts us. We may become obsessed with dogma or ascension, but the power of the descent is too subtle and too strong to be ignored. It is not even a matter of attitude but a question of perception—the perception that light belongs in darkness, clarity in obscurity, that darkness can't be rejected for the sake of light—because everything contains its opposite.

Inanna symbolizes that feeling-capacity that comes with the inner knowing of life as a changing process. The feeling calls us to evaluate afresh the structures of our life and community. She is not afraid, and does not resist change and the turmoil it brings. But her receptivity is active. For her time, the goddess Inanna (her Semitic name is Ishtar) provides a many-faceted symbolic image of the feminine beyond the merely maternal. Like Demeter, she is an image of impersonal fertility. She is also from the beginning a goddess of the heavens, of gentle rains and terrible storms and floods. She is called "queen of heaven" and the "morning and evening star," awakening life and setting it to rest, ushering in or out her brother, the moon god, and her father, the sun god.

She represents those liminal intermediate regions and energies that cannot be contained or made certain and secure. She is consciousness of transition and places of intersection and creativity—all in human consciousness that is flexible, courageous, and never certain for very long.

Most of what Inanna represented for the Sumerians has since been exiled. Most of the qualities of the upper-world goddess have been desacralized or taken over by masculine divinities, or have been overly idealized by the patriarchal moral and esthetic codes. I believe this is one reason why the passionate, powerful, independent, self-willed feminine, the ambitious, regal, many-sided feminine, is now erupting through dark times in both males and females as a wrathful, withdrawn, wild, sad, grief-ridden depression.

To me, this is the key point: The descent is not, as our culture suggests, an aberration, an illness, or a running-off-the-rails. It is a vital, sacred, and irreplaceable part of human wholeness. I can think of no better example of how modern culture has lost its way than in the describing of "taboo" as told by Joseph Campbell. "The term *taboo* comes from an ancient tribal island culture. In the sacred rites of initiation, young men were required to spend extended periods of time outside the protection of the tribe. This meant living beyond the markers that indicated the boundary of tribal protection. Those markers were called *tabu*."

This underscores the wisdom we have lost: for while it is necessary for social order that we live within the boundaries of social convention, it is absolutely crucial that we also become familiar with the "demons" that lie beyond those boundaries. When we befriend our demons, we discover that they are nothing other than unrecognized angels—and that potent gifts await us if we can but follow them into the dark light.

13

"You're Worth It"

Jennifer L. Holder

> I came to view my boyfriend's depression as
> sacred, a rite of passage that he needed to go
> through, that couldn't be wished or encouraged
> or cheered away. I set a rule for myself—never
> ask him to be different than he is. So I focused
> on the physical comforts, on offering him a
> spacious presence so that while he often pushed
> me away, he could still know I was there, that I
> loved him, and that he was worth it—not only
> to me, but to himself. He could keep going.

In the final stages of compiling this anthology with Tami Simon, as I marveled at the magic of this chorus speaking in such harmony, I began to feel the absence of one voice. Depression is an experience that affects its sufferers deeply, yes, but we cannot offer its full expression without addressing the way it ripples in the lives of others. In my life, personally, I have only had light dips into depression, but I love a man who has almost drowned in its depths. Journeying alongside him through the years has offered profound lessons in compassion, gentleness, fortitude, and patience. With his depression, every time I lose touch with these virtues I receive a sharp and painful reminder from him, like the smack of a Zen teacher's stick, and I jerk back awake. He is my teacher, and just as he is my companion, so is his depression.

I do not have a well-known voice, nor am I a spiritual teacher, but in the two years it has taken to compile this radical compendium of redefinition, I have engaged its contents within the world built by me and my consort. And so, I offer my story as a kind of baseline drumbeat to encourage and maybe even bolster the other ground-stabilizers who love people with depression. While we wish the best for them—whatever "best" might be—at heart, we really want them to be happy. I think it's okay to wish that, even if we never dare to voice it in fear of the reprimand we might receive from the depths of our loved one's misery.

My boyfriend's depression was a presence in our relationship from the start. When, three years before we met, his father died suddenly, he was laid off, and a longtime girlfriend left him, he dove deep enough to desire the nothingness of death. Amazingly, he avoided the lures of rafters and tailpipes and triggers, and kept his life together. With the help of antidepressants and a psychologist, one foot after the other he lived out his days, and in the months before our first date, he had the energy to find a more positive workplace environment for himself. But his mother had just been diagnosed with cancer and was starting treatment. In other words, he was exhausted by treading water for so long, and he knew—but didn't voice—that he would continue to do so for a long time to come.

I think back to my first impressions of him. He was this fascinating paradox to me. An engaging and informed conversationalist, a sensualist who cooked culinary masterpieces, a book lover who read voraciously, a deep thinker who cared strongly and passionately about the state of the world and humanity. He definitely had the energy to charm me, which was good because his presence impacted me enough to keep me coming back. But at the same time, he would suddenly cancel dates, incapacitated by his mood. We would make plans and I would arrive at his house to find him deeply asleep on the couch, a process it took him hours to complete and then hours to fully awaken from. When asked by my friends why I stayed with him, as challenging as the daily navigation of moods and energy and his mother's illness was, I had no answer. It wasn't something rational I could easily express. My friends told me to find someone "together," someone "fun," someone with whom I could just enjoy a good time.

I faced them down with distrust: Would they leave me if I didn't provide those things for them? Was my value only found in what I could contribute to their entertainment?

I used to say to him frequently, "You're worth it." I think that was the only thing I ever said that would bring him great peace.

I remember standing outside a bar where Sounds True was holding its winter holiday party. One of my coworkers had, kind of playfully, kind of aggressively, told him that he better be good to me. Well, that day he had learned that his favorite aunt had died, and couldn't handle the emotional challenge my coworker presented. I managed to chase him as he ran out the door, and while shivering in my dress and telling him that he could feel free to go home, I said, "My care is unconditional." I meant it. Through the years, we have left parties, cancelled events, and taken long naps instead of going skiing as we'd planned. He struggles to get out of bed in the mornings, so every single day I bring him a steaming mug of coffee, set it on the bedside table, and kiss or cuddle him awake so that his first encounter with the world is filled with kindness.

When he dutifully visited his mother, he would return unable to talk. I would have stocked his pantry and fridge with food so he wouldn't have to leave the house for days as he recovered. I quietly replaced empty tissue boxes and provided frames for the photos he dug up of his mother. These gestures always seemed more profound and effective than talking about things. He made it sharply clear he didn't want to "process" or to seek deeper meaning or to do any self-development work of any kind. But, after Tami came to me with the idea for this anthology, I came across and gave him the book *The Mindful Way through Depression*. He read fifty pages and learned how he could stop the endless, repeating thought train that only led to inertia and misery. We were both amazed at the effect—suddenly, life activities became easier to engage in. He started cooking more, his conversation brightened, and he became more interested in meditation practice. And when he decided he was ready to wean himself off the antidepressants, we both went through an intense and precarious roller coaster, but he did it.

As is his style, he began to read voraciously about Buddhism. He even incorporated meditation practice and mindfulness into his life. But here's the thing: I had to wait until it hooked his attention, independent of me. I am a longtime Buddhist practitioner; I know the amazing things a meditation practice can do to cultivate wellbeing—especially its power to cut rumination, to facilitate letting go of habits that hold us back, memories that haunt us, even painful emotions in the moments they arise. But all of those tools served only to make my own patience possible, to fortify my own ongoing feelings of happiness. All that experience only helped me hold my own seat—it meant nothing to my boyfriend until he connected with it of his own volition.

It's odd to me to think back on those years and realize I was happy. I guess I made a conscious decision that I was going to devote most of my energy to cultivating our relationship—and, yes, that often meant navigating his moods. There was this feeling that I had lived plenty of time for myself—I had travelled the world in my twenties, done extensive meditation retreats, built my career as a book editor, and was working in a stable and supportive environment. So I had the resources to be there for him. Why do it? Because as a living, breathing, kind man with traits I admired and a style I could really relate with, he was worth it.

Also, through the ups and downs of my own journey through the years, I had come to realize that there is no other way life should be. Why bind ourselves to the idea of what happiness should look like? Why think that it's all fun and games, that love is an ecstatic and blissful union all the time, that life should feel easy, and practicalities always flow effortlessly? I had found that to be totally unrealistic in my own life, so I didn't apply that to my life with him. I rejoiced with food and wine when he did; I went back to my house when he couldn't bear my presence; I kept silent about topics meaningful to me when he couldn't handle the emotions they brought up.

But most importantly, as I was working with the content that came our way from the contributors to this anthology, I came to view his depression as sacred, a rite of passage that he needed to go through, that couldn't be wished or encouraged or cheered away. I set a rule for myself—never ask him to be different than he is. So I focused on the physical comforts, on offering him a spacious presence so that while he often pushed me away, he could still know I was there, that I loved him, and that he was worth it—not only to me, but to himself. He could keep going.

I won't let this general, sweeping overview convey the sense that this was easy for me. It wasn't. Sometimes, I was challenged to my bones. I got totally emotional. I refused to talk to him for stretches, just to get a break. I constantly stumbled around, trying to find some kind of handhold on his emotional state so that I could offer him what he needed in that moment—but more often than not, he offered me nothing to grip. It was groundless and ever shifting, as unpredictable and heartrending as building a house on the San Andreas Fault. All in all, it was great training in being genuinely human.

Then, two days after my birthday, he drove to see his mother and didn't come back for six weeks. He had taken a copy of Joseph Goldstein's book *Mindfulness* with him, and I have since seen the dog-eared pages and underlines and even some wavy pages that may have become wet with tears. He read it during the long nights at her bedside, and in the few moments he had to himself, he meditated before a little statue of the Buddha that I lent him and that he set in a dollhouse in the bedroom he occupied. We texted frequently, and this is when he became receptive to my whispers. I could suddenly offer guidance and perspective and insight. He could bring me his challenges, and I could ask him questions until he made what he felt to be the right decisions. These were decisions like when to call hospice and when to inject that final, comforting but horrifying, goodbye morphine dose. At such a distance, it was as if I became a part of his inner world.

It has now been nine months since his mother died. And I will tell you that the road on the other side of depression continues to be challenging. He has gone through a tremendous inner journey, and while he isn't chronically depressed anymore, for a while he couldn't quite decide who he was or what he wanted. He would sometimes try on old habits, like putting on an old pair of pants, and get upset when they didn't fit anymore. He grew impatient for all the newly emerging dreams and visions for his life to come to fruition right away, and the disappointment was huge when the circumstances and conditions didn't fit. He became very demanding of me, insisting that I change for the better. An idealism about what life should be like, post-depression, when daily challenges are objectively small but in reality still quite painful, made him intolerant of darker emotions in both of us. And when these dark states arise, as they can with force when suppressed, the ground drops out from under him and his thoughts turn once again to death.

I love this man. We have been through so much together, and we are still journeying with depression. Now, it takes the form of a resistance to sadness that is close to terror. It came up most clearly when we went on a beautiful lakeside vacation for total rest and relaxation. For ten days we read, cooked, talked, canoed, and played board games as we listened to the wind in the trees, watched waves on the lake, and felt clouds come and go. I adored the rustic cabin and the peace we found there. So, naturally to me, I was sad to leave. He humored me for a while and was kind about it—until it began to feel threatening to his own wellbeing somehow. What was to me a sweet melancholia, an honoring of the place and the experience, and a visceral implanting of good memories, to him threatened the joy of the entire vacation. I have noticed how sadness makes him jump out of his skin. But I understand. So recently, the sadness was completely overwhelming and it left a mark of trauma. I think he's afraid that if it goes beyond a certain point it will swell into another devastating flood.

A question lingers for me: it's often easy to wish that all beings be happy, but how do we express our wish for our depressed loved one to be happy? Our cheerfulness, our efforts to distract, and the small and big ways we try to help can be rejected outright. We take the lashes because we know that it is the mood speaking. At times, we can understand why the feelings are so thick, because there is a reason; at other times, it's as much a mystery to the sufferer as it is to us. But my bedrock to stand on—especially when my boyfriend has no ground under his feet—is a mix of the respect I feel for him and his journey, the high value of his inherent worth as a human being, and the love

I feel. I find that love is a fuel for my caregiving that provides amazing mileage. This helps me let go, over and over again, to return to my own sense of journey as I train in the skillful means of offering genuine, openhearted presence to someone in pain. May what I have learned come in handy when applied to the great project of liberating all beings from suffering.

14

A Spiritual Response
to Our Times

Christina Baldwin

People come to me, pull me aside, and urgently
whisper: "What do I do with my grief for the state
of the world? How can I not fall into despair?"
Their questions, and particularly their trust that
I know what they are talking about, invites me to
see my own depression as a donation of personal
experience to the learning of the whole.

In the web of life, everything is interconnected: my life and the world's
life are inextricably linked. I understand that we might not make it
through the crises in which we find ourselves *and* I believe that life is
incredibly glorious anyway. I am a person in love with Nature *and* one
who suffers outrage at our collective behavior toward its miraculous
intricacies. I am a person in love with humanity's goodness *and* also
able to look into the bleak corners where children are abused, women
raped, men humiliated and tortured. I draw sustenance from my belief
that beauty balances horror, and that we are more good than evil. I let
myself be lifted up; I let myself be broken open.

I live in one of the world's beautiful places, on an island in Puget
Sound, just north of Seattle, Washington. My cliff-side neighborhood
faces west, where across ten miles of salt water I can daily watch the
play of weather over Olympic National Park and its mountain peaks. I
have stood at my kitchen window and watched a pod of orcas chasing

salmon on the currents, watched eagles swoop up the gap between trees that is our gravel road so close I could see the glint in their eyes. There are days when the water becomes floating diamonds and the mountains a black jawline topped with white teeth. Standing down on the beach below my house, I fall to my knees in awe. I cry out at the beauty, sing made-up tunes of thankfulness, and know such ecstasy that it is almost a sexual explosion, such embodiment of my earthly being. Isn't the world worthy of adoration?

I live in one of the world's beautiful places, on an island in Puget Sound where the great old forests have been felled to build Seattle, and the second-growth trees are carried off the island by ferry on long-bed hearses on their way to becoming plywood and toilet paper. From my kitchen window, I can see how the clear-cuts rise over the foothills, stopping only at the boundary of the national park. I have seen the carcass of a starved grey whale roll in the surf, its fragile food chain interrupted. I have held the body of an eagle with a bullet hole in its breast. There are days when the fog rolls in so thick I can barely see the edge of my lawn, and standing down on the beach below my house, I fall to my knees in despair. I cry over the beauty we are losing, sing made-up tunes of lament, and know such sadness that my heart breaks in my chest, such embodiment of the consequences that my species wreaks on the planet. Isn't the world worthy of sorrow?

I live with the tension of knowing the serenity of my home environment is temporary. I can take joy in it—and I do; I can mourn the erosion of its delicate balance—and I do. Holding this balance is a rigorous and ongoing spiritual practice: sometimes I vacillate between denial and despair.

There are rooms in my mind full of such sorrow I do not want to enter. Yet all my life, the doors to those rooms are blown open again and again by the world's suffering: the Cuban Missile Crisis, the Vietnam War, Chernobyl, 9/11, the tsunamis, typhoons, hurricanes, earthquakes, fires, the relentless erosion of ordinary human life and honorable livelihood. There is the suffering caused by Nature, and the suffering we cause Nature.

Standing in the many mansions of my mind, I can usually maintain a balance and spiritual centeredness. But sometimes world events and catastrophes catch me by surprise, exploding in my heart. My first initiation into the world's impact on my personal life occurred when I was a junior in high school, editor of the school paper, working up the courage to ask a boy to the Sadie Hawkins Day dance. On October 15, 1962, all my teenage priorities suddenly changed during a historic event now called the "Cuban Missile Crisis," a standoff between the governments of the United States and the Soviet Union. For thirteen days, the fate of the world hung in a balance between these two powers: both countries poised with fingers itching on the nuclear buttons of World War III. What do you do if you are one Midwestern American teenager helpless on the world stage?

I took a metal banker's box out of our basement, filled it with my diary, a copy of Anne Frank's diary, my Bible, some photos of family and our house, a few newspaper clippings, and a note to the future. I buried the box in the woods behind our yard. Then I sneaked back into the house and set the table for supper, did my homework, went to school the next morning. I tried to cope with the façade of ordinary routine while the possibility that we might all be living at the gates of nuclear holocaust played on the screen of my mind. I remember sitting in classes hearing this silent scream in the back of my mind: "Is this really how you want to spend your final moments? Isn't there anybody willing to talk about this?"

We lived, but we didn't talk about it. I dug up the banker's box, put away my things, told no one. But my expectations about living were irrevocably changed. Life was not a guarantee. In the comfortable trappings of middle-class privilege, nothing around me looked different, but I was profoundly changed. I walked out of my childhood and into the complexities of the world, unable to retreat into "not knowing."

Over the decades since, I have vacillated many times between denial and despair, and come again and again to a sense of balance that has allowed me to carry on. I assumed I had accumulated enough resilience and had enough belief in the value of my life work that I could buffer myself from despondency. Then one April day in 2010, when the drilling platform Deepwater Horizon exploded in the Gulf of Mexico and news of the oil spill spread, my heart was hit so hard my protective shell shattered. In the following weeks, as the bodies of birds and animals rolled dead in the surf and the water continued to cloud with heavy sludge, I lost control of my emotional containment. I was spewing despair just like the broken pipe head was spewing oil. It didn't look like either of us was going to "get better" any time soon.

This particular world disaster coincided with a personal, age-related sense that at sixty-four years old I was rounding the curve and heading into the last stretch of a long, highly self-designed writing and teaching career. My partner and I had just released a co-authored book and were busy teaching, promoting the book, flying around using up fossil fuel. My dog died that June. I began three years of frozen shoulder syndrome—first left, then right. I fell and bruised bones in my foot. I was humbled, hobbled, exhausted.

Imagining myself at this point in my life, at the peak of my craft, I expected myself to exude confidence, hold spiritual leadership, offer guidance, and come through on the promise that the new book would help change the world. So I suffered as privately as I could. My partner knew. She could feel the loss of heart, the tamped-down energy, the struggle to stay steady in a public self. I didn't want this to be *the end*, but I didn't have any idea how to go on.

In the pages of my journal, I wrote out the private questioning. The voice in the back of my mind was chanting, "I am so done . . . " It scared me: what does that mean? I patted my body reassuringly, telling myself, "No cancer, no accidents, no car crashes . . . " How can part of myself give up? What is she giving up? What is she done with?

This wasn't clinical depression; it didn't fit a category. The *Random House Dictionary of the English Language* defines clinical depression as "sadness greater and more prolonged than that warranted by any objective reason." My psychological storm felt totally warranted. As a member of a species psychopathically destroying its social structures and biosphere, isn't grief reasonable? Isn't rage appropriate? I didn't want medication; I wanted stamina to endure and learn.

In long-ago studies of psychology, I learned to define despair as "a breakdown in dialogue between the self and the world." To maintain psychological health, the self needs to feel that it can negotiate life conditions and ameliorate circumstances, even in the midst of trauma. Individuals who manage to maintain this sense of negotiation can often live through even incredibly cruel or challenging experiences with psychological resilience. We hear powerful survival tales—from prisoners of war, refugees, torture victims, survivors of accidents and illness—who found some tiny area of self-empowerment that they could focus on and construct their rock to stand on. If they lost this point of empowerment, or if their tormentors understood what this was and removed it, their pain overwhelmed them and their resilience collapsed.

Somehow, in the ongoing roll call of disasters, this particular oil spill removed my rock of resilience. I could not hold the balance any longer; could not see both beauty and disaster, both joy and despair. I became a pelican, soaked in oil.

Eighty-seven days later, on July 12, 2010, British Petroleum Corporation announced it had successfully capped the well. Good news, but not the end of the crisis for the Gulf—or for me. My heart remained tarred and feathered. I had unleashed a powerful crisis in myself, and I couldn't turn it off. A friend listening to me on the phone said simply, "I think you need to let yourself die. You are being reborn." I wrote it boldface in my journal—not afraid of the instruction, though not sure how to allow such a thing. It is hard to see the creative transformation of depression while fighting to stay afloat in the black ooze.

In late August of that year, on a three-day retreat wandering the wild edge of the Pacific coast, I shouted into the surf's roar, "What do you want from me?" I grabbed my despair by the throat, shook it hard. Freed by my aloneness in the landscape, I stormed along the empty beach. "I am not some f-king donkey for you to work to death!" I shouted to the sea and sky, my voice as raucous as the gulls. "People have spent their whole lives in activism and protest, seeking alternatives to our destructive path. So why are corporations and governments still taking such risks with the beloved biosphere? Why, at the end of four decades, are things worse?"

And after a while, from the white noise of the sea I heard a quiet voice calmly say:

> I am asking you to keep faith with life. I am
> asking you to not collapse into fear, depression,
> denial, or even into anguish. I am asking you to
> refuse to surrender to anything that immobilizes
> you, for I still have need of you.

I sat down on a driftwood log to transcribe into the journal what I heard with my inner ear. The voice continued to whisper:

> I am asking you to take care of yourself, to listen
> carefully to your body, mind, and spirit so that you
> remain a healthy and clear vessel for me. I am asking
> you to rebuild your spiritual stamina so that we can be
> in dialogue about what remains yours to do.
>   Where you are now is a continuation of the dialogue
> we have been in all your life. You have wearied yourself
> in the journey and fallen into the well of despair. I am
> sorry, and you will recover. Humanity is so out of balance
> with nature that the laws of nature are correcting that
> imbalance. Trust the pattern even though you cannot
> see its wholeness. Part of what life still wants from you
> is your capacity for both joy and sorrow in this situation.
> Be one who notices, who makes story; one who offers
> context and pattern and helps create meaning so that
> people can move forward together.

I was crying—wetting the heart. I whispered my mantra of seven whispers—a prayer I had been reciting since 1999.

> If Thou will have me, what I want most in the remaining
> decades of my life is to be able to serve the village as
> its wise old woman, to know what to do because I am

listening to You and Your instructions. I want to be true
to the litany of my heart: to maintain peace of mind, to
move at the pace of guidance, to practice certainty of
purpose, to surrender to surprise, to ask for what I need
and offer what I can, to love the folks in front of me,
and to return to the world. This is my prayer, my prayer,
my long-whispered prayer.

Time passed. Silence and surf. A new puppy rested at my feet watching me. I felt the sludge of months lift off me. I felt the salt of the sea mingle with my tears. My hand was cramped from writing, and the journal was creased with sand. I stretched the wings of my being.

Yes. Yes, I will. Yes.

Such a small word: *yes, si, oui, ja, da, namah, shi, hai.* It seems every language makes saying "yes" something simple, a roll off the tongue. Saying "yes" is like looking through a keyhole into a room full of future possibilities: everything looks in place, organized and manageable. However, once we open the door to what we've said "yes" to, the room is far bigger, less organized, and more unmanageable than anticipated. We will have to grow in order to inhabit our "yes."

I never actually intended to speak of this deep dive to anyone, but since then it is as though I smell of tar, and cleanser, and the salted air of release. People come to me, pull me aside, and urgently whisper: "What do I do with my grief for the state of the world? How can I not fall into despair?" Their questions, and particularly their trust that I will know what they are talking about, invites me to see my dark swim as a donation of personal experience to the learning of the whole.

As I write this, the nuclear power plant at Fukushima, nearly destroyed by the March 2011 tsunami that struck northern Japan, continues to face an extremely tenuous situation that threatens global catastrophe. Starting in November 2013, technicians began attempting to move the spent fuel rods of Reactor 4 to "a safer location." Meanwhile, 300 tons of contaminated water a day continued to seep into the ground and sea. A disaster at the plant could release 14,000 times more radioactivity than Hiroshima, and the only plan in place is to prepare for several hundred years of maintenance with the hope that future technology will lead to a solution.

The beautiful place where I live is directly in the path of atomic drift—by air and ocean currents. A recent headline read, "Not since the Cuban Missile Crisis has the world been this close to nuclear disaster." We come full circle.

I cannot bury a stash of more than one hundred volumes of my journal in the woods, hoping that the future will find my story valuable. I cannot clean the tar off my feathers, attempting to leave trauma behind. I am standing on the western shore of my country and in the autumn of my life. I cannot run from this invisible threat: there is no place to go. I let myself be lifted up. I stand in place—matured, humbled, ready to do my part within the ineffable sorrow of my times. I let myself be broken open.

The word *ineffable* evokes those emotions that cannot be spoken about in daily routines. The word comes from the Latin *inefabilis* and is defined as:

1. incapable of being described in words; inexpressible
2. not to be spoken because of its sacredness; unutterable

We who have come through depression and stand with the sacred pearl it offers exude a faint scent of salty survival that attracts others who are seeking to find their way. We pull each other aside and whisper. We try to bring the ineffable into words. We seek to discover what our roles are now that we have survived and reclaimed our place in the new day of our lives.

And I ask myself over and over: *Is this not what we have been preparing for all along, the dawn of a new day?* That day dawns, and we are made ready by the fact of our survival. That day dawns, and we are made ready by our capacity to keep finding a rock to stand on, even when it's just a pebble. That day dawns, and our fate remains complex and uncertain. Fukushima is yet another opportunity for us to stand with ineffable sorrow in our hearts and with determination to move forward anyway, to get to work on creating a fresh world.

In Nature, nothing is wasted, so I must believe that in our own nature as human beings, nothing is wasted either. If depression is a natural part of life, then those of us who have been thrown into the well of ineffable sorrow have a spiritual obligation to share our experience and the story we have made from the journey. Reframing depression is an essential skill for our survival in these times. We are not falling apart for no good reason; we are falling apart so that we might come back together stronger in our broken-open places. As more and more people take their hit to the heart, however it presents itself, we serve as one another's guides. We are the ones who can say, "I have been this way and there is a way through."

In Nature, the poison and the antidote grow in proximity to one another: for poison ivy there is spotted jewelweed. For bee sting, there is honey. The voice of guidance that calmed my heart that day I was shouting down the sea probably saved my life. Until that moment, I did not know that my despair and the way through the despair were growing in proximity within me. Somehow I managed to flip from rage to grace. This capacity is in us, and manifests over and over: it is our negotiation point with the world—inner and outer. Whatever parts of the psyche are blown open, we carry the antidote: the arduous journey is to recognize and access it. We are falling apart individually because we need to become collectively prepared. We are falling apart so that we might discover in ourselves the pearl of collective resilience and use it to become as strong as Nature needs us to be.

In Nature, nothing is wasted. In our own natures, nothing is wasted. Sorrow is an initiation. Sorrow is a gateway into stamina. I don't know what comes now. I don't know what will be required of you and me in the remaining decades of our lives. I know that touching the dark ooze of my own psyche was part of what I needed to know so that I was no longer afraid of it; respectful, yes, but not phobic, not avoidant. Touching down and swimming up, I can listen to you and not be afraid of your chaos; respectful, yes, but not phobic, not avoidant. We can receive one another, speak our truths, make space for our differences, choose wise action.

It is awful and awe full to get up every morning, raise the shades, and see if the world as I count on it is still holding steady. I make a cup of tea. I sit in the corner bench in my living room and watch the day rise. My beloved sits alongside: We talk quietly about matters of the heart. We set our intentions into the day. The dog is curled at our feet. The wind blows in from the west. The tides and currents swirl Pacific waters, depositing a ragged line of seaweed and Japanese plastic along my beach.

We do not know what's coming. Life is beautiful anyway.

15

Depression as Initiation

An Interview with Sandra Ingerman

I can be experiencing a place where everything
seems empty to me and there's no God, there's no
spirit, there is nothing. And at the same time there
is an invisible process going on inside of me that
ends up creating something new—a new state
of awareness, a new state of spiritual awakening,
more gifts for me to use to help other people who
are traveling in these same waters.

Tami Simon   How do you understand depression from a shamanic perspective?

Sandra Ingerman   From a shamanic point of view, depression—as well as any form of what our culture labels "mental illness"—has been historically viewed as a rite of passage into a spiritual state of being. In a shamanic culture, when someone was in a depressed state the community would really hold a supportive space for that person during that time because they knew it was a very important initiation. From a shamanic point of view, depression is seen as an initiation.

TS   For many who are stuck in depression for quite a long time, it may not feel like a rite of passage or initiation.

SI   From a shamanic point of view, there are different stages in our lives. Depression, too, moves in different stages, where a person emerges, being reborn into a new state, sometimes only to cycle back into depression at a later time.

In any initiation, there is a process of ego dissolution and disintegration that occurs, a dismemberment process, in which we lose a sense of self, identity, and personality. During this disintegration, we might enter into the void: a state of nothingness where those in depression feel as if it's all darkness, that there's nothing—no God, no spirit, no anything.

From a Buddhist perspective, the void is a place of emptiness, but also of fullness. The void is the territory that is prior to matter and form and filled with unlimited potential. It's a very rich place, but when you're depressed this void can seem very empty. It is out of this void that a new birth comes, what in shamanism we would call "the illumination," the reemergence of being reconstructed. It is a process through which we release parts of our old stories and parts of our personality that no longer serve us. We become reconstructed into a healthier body, a stronger mind, and a stronger soul. We might return with a new sense of direction and a new set of values. From this state, we receive new insights and gain compassion for others. We let go of old beliefs, old ways of living, and personality traits so we open to a new, expanded awareness of consciousness and to a new level of awareness.

There are two different phases of depression in shamanism: the dismemberment phase, in which you experience the darkness; and then the re-memberment and reemergence phase, in which you are reborn into the light. Because, in the first phase, the personality is annihilated on an emotional level, it requires spiritual strength to make it through, to be initiated. Then, on the other side, it can also be difficult to reemerge and find oneself completely transformed. This can create problems for a person because when they emerge, it feels like they have new skin. Coming out of a deep state of depression can be a fragile and vulnerable time in a person's life, because it's like putting on clothes that all of a sudden no longer fit. The person is transformed, and time is needed to feel comfortable among their friends, their coworkers, and in the world. This can lead to feelings of isolation. It can take a while to get used to being in that new skin—creating new boundaries and a new way of navigating through life.

Another way of looking at depression from a shamanic point of view is to understand that a person who has gone deep into a depressed state can emerge and be seen as a "wounded healer." The deep wound they possess provides a shamanic practitioner with the compassion he or she needs to be able to heal and to hold space for any type of suffering. When you feel like you possess an open wound, you can't close down to the suffering of others. For some people, as has been the case in my life, depression can be a lifelong journey that can keep you in a state of compassion so that you can hold space for others—for a client, for a community, or for anything that a person might be going through.

Also, as an initiate is dismembered, he or she can have a numinous experience of unity consciousness, leading the initiate to emerge with psychic and healing gifts.

TS   How does a person increase the spiritual strength that is required to make it through depression?

SI   In my own depression, at times suicidal and in some very dark states, the mantra I used was, "The strength of my spirit will carry me through." I used this mantra for over a month as I lay in bed in a fetal position. Even though one of my helping spirits told me it was an initiation, I was convinced I would not make it through. Her response was, "If you thought you were going to live through this, it wouldn't be an initiation."

Through surviving an initiation, we learn how to live. Just as how physical strength is developed, we start with a five-pound weight, move to a seven-pound weight, and then on to a ten-pound weight. As we survive each new challenge, strength develops. No matter how deep your depression is, if you are still alive, you are surviving the depths of that experience, and each time you move through a phase of depression, you become stronger.

The other mantra I used during this time was, "The only way out is through." During very difficult states, such as profound depression, your mind is annihilated and it is your spirit that holds you . . . All of the ordinary ways of thinking of yourself and your life are not helpful in powering through. It is an invisible part of ourselves that carries us through these challenging times, a part of ourselves we're not ordinarily aware of that is actually the vessel which holds us as we go through the storm.

TS   When did depression first come into your life, and how has this experience been for you?

SI   I started getting depressed when I was about thirteen years old. I was unaware of the cause at the time, but I feel it's some part of my spiritual destiny, or the shamanic path of the wounded healer. In my twenties, I had a difficult time managing it, and I thought about committing myself to a mental institution. After considering all of the implications of doing so, I decided to ride out the storm. When I began practicing shamanism, my main guardian spirit came to me in a journey—not while I was depressed, because I can't journey for myself when I'm depressed—and he said, "You're straddling two worlds. We don't really care which one you choose, but you have to choose one—you either have to choose life or you have to choose death. One day you want to be here and one day you don't want to be here. You can't keep going back and forth." He asked me to choose if I wanted to live or if I wanted to die. I decided I wanted to live.

After that, my depression took on a different character. It wasn't that I didn't feel depression anymore, but there was more movement on my part to learn how to be more functional with my depressed feelings. For example, I could be having dinner with a friend or teaching a workshop and I could be feeling internally quite depressed, but those around me wouldn't know the state I was in. The best and strongest tool I've developed is to just observe the state of depression without trying to change it in any way—to be with the depression and not to "whine" about it.

There were phases in my life in which I did need community to hold space for me; I wanted people in my life who I knew were not going to ask me if I wanted help. When you're in a depressed state, it is not helpful to hear, "What can I do to help you?" or "Don't worry about it, you're going to make it through." Because when you're in a depressed state, you don't know if you're going to make it through—so when somebody says, "You're going to look back on this time and you're going to laugh," it's like hearing nails scratching on a black-board. Nobody truly knows whether you're going to make it through. You might not make it through. That's a reality. For me it was most helpful to have friends willing to just listen and hold the space for me while I was in a dark state. This was a strong anchor for me. Eventually, I strengthened into being able to hold this space for myself.

When I work with others who are depressed, I try to help them to stay with what is and just to observe that space, not trying to do anything about it. For me, this is one of the strongest tools and per-haps the only reason I'm alive today—being able to hold the space of acceptance.

TS   Many describe the journey of depression as something they went through for a period of a few years, and then came out of. For you, though, it sounds as if depression is a lifelong experience that comes and goes.

SI   Yes, absolutely. After I had my first soul retrieval in my early forties, for a couple of years or so I came out of my depression. It was like some sort of miraculous cure. And then, after a couple of years, the experience of depression came back, but with a different flavor.

Depression has become a very rich spiritual state for me, and is something I've come to accept. I do ride many beautiful waves of living a life filled with joy. At the same time, at the age of sixty-one, I can say I've lived much of my life in a state of depression. I've accepted that this is the way I'm going to be riding through my life, which helps me to forgive myself and to not judge myself about it. I just stay with what is. But I do have to say, despite the fact that it is a rich and deep experience, it is not comfortable and I wouldn't say that I enjoy it. I don't look forward to diving into a dark state, but it's where my creativity comes from. It's a place where nothing's happening, but everything's happening at the same time, just like the void is empty but it's also full. I can be experiencing a place where everything seems empty to me and there's no God, there's no spirit, there is nothing, and at the same time there is an invisible process going on inside of me that ends up creating something new—a new state of awareness, a new state of spiritual awakening, more gifts for me to use to help other people—people who are traveling in these same waters. In some ways, nobody can get you out of those waters, but there are certain tools and ways of holding space for others that can be really helpful for them. I do share shamanic practices that provide tools to help people navigate the waves of depression and inspire passion for life.

TS   Can you say more about this link in your experience between depression and creativity?

SI   When you plant something in the ground, there is an invisible process that happens as a seed starts to germinate. Prior to germination, there is something that goes on in the darkness of the earth that is an invisible state before growth starts to happen. It's like the season of winter, during which it seems like nothing is happening, but in fact there is a natural process going on to promote growth. It goes back to the initiation state in shamanism of complete disintegration, when one goes into the void before the re-memberment, reconstruction, and illumination can happen. There is a cycle of winter that happens in growth, when it seems nothing's happening, but there is something potent going on. It's not a conscious process.

TS   What is a person being initiated into through depression?

SI   In my experience, what starts to happen is that who you think you are—the surface of your ego and personality—is carved away so that the depth of your spirit can shine through. It's like you're being polished through a sculpting process in which you lose a part of your personality, part of your characteristics. As you're being polished, you keep evolving into a more spiritual being, because you've let go of some of the personality you've been attached to throughout your life and discover your authentic self.

TS   How do you see soul retrieval in relationship to depression? Could it possibly serve as a cure for some people?

SI   Yes, I've worked with many clients who completely shifted out of a state of depression after a soul retrieval. When used in conjunction with making positive life changes, soul retrieval can be very effective in treating depression. Soul loss is a classic diagnosis of illness from a shamanic point of view. The shamanic definition of "soul" is that it is our essence, that part of us which keeps us alive. Whenever we experience an emotional or physical trauma in life, a part of our soul separates from our body in order to survive the experience. For this reason, I always talk about soul loss as our psyche's way of surviving a trauma.

For example, if someone is about to be in a head-on car collision, or beaten, or abused, this can trigger a self-protection mechanism in which part of his or her soul flees the body while the trauma is occurring. This is so they won't have to experience the full impact of the pain. From a shamanic point of view, shock is soul loss in which we separate from the body so that we don't feel the full impact of the traumatic event.

Classic symptoms of soul loss are dissociation, depression, suicidal tendencies, not wanting to be here, not feeling like you fit in to life, and so forth. PTSD, immune-deficiency illnesses, and addictions are symptoms of soul loss. Any time someone says they don't feel the same since a trauma, this would be a sign that soul loss has occurred. People describe not feeling completely whole. So, yes, there are people who can be completely cured with a soul retrieval, a process by which a shamanic practitioner brings back and returns the lost soul part to the physical body.

TS   In what ways do you think your experiences of depression have contributed to the development of wisdom within you?

SI   To start, my depression keeps me from living on a superficial level. I do go to what I consider very deep, rich, spiritual states and, again, through every phase of disintegration, there come deeper states of illumination. The darkness takes us to the depths of consciousness, while the light takes us to states of further bliss. The deeper that we can go, the more illumination we can receive. The reemergence catalyzes a state of wisdom and creativity, and also brings me to a place of surrender and acceptance. I find that for myself when I can really hang in there in a place of surrender and accept what is, there's always wisdom that comes from that.

TS   In what way do you feel that these dark periods of initiation are an important part of your destiny?

SI   I've explored this question quite a bit. I do feel it is my destiny to be on a spiritual path and to work with people and offer help during challenging times. When I've been "too happy," it becomes difficult for me to maintain a deep compassionate state toward some of the dark places that my clients and students can go. During such times, I have to really work at being compassionate, because there's a part of me that moves into the thought process, "Oh, you can change this state, this is all illusion." On some level, of course, it *is* all illusion. Depression doesn't really exist on a spiritual level, yet everything we go through—all the pain and suffering we go through on a physical level—is real to us. However, on a spiritual level, it's *not* real, and when I find that I'm in a very light, happy state, it's hard for me to be able to really stay in a place of compassion while people around me are suffering. Depression is like an open wound that keeps me compassionate—and I accept that. I'm at a place in my life where, sure, I would love for things to be different, but this is what's happening, and I am committed to staying with what's happening, knowing that I have the internal tools to ride out whatever storm is going on.

I have always known that my depression was part of something going on spiritually for me, which is why I never sought out help from traditional psychotherapy or have taken any medication for it. It's kept me searching on a spiritual level, going deeper, and gaining spiritual strength, because that's what keeps me alive. In this way, depression has been the fuel that keeps me on my spiritual path.

TS   Even though neither God nor your helping spirits have been able to remove depression from your life, somehow your faith has been kept alive.

SI   Yes, I've always had my faith. Some people I know who have been diagnosed with cancer, for example, who are on a spiritual path, will say, "I've done my spiritual practice. I've done everything right. Why did this happen to me?" For me, I've always had faith that whatever is happening is what needs to be happening. There's a church I pass every day that posts sayings, and one really stood out for me. It said, "If God seems far away, who moved?" This is so true. I know my spirits are always there and God has always been there, and when I move into those places of depression, *they* don't move away from me; I move away from them. Our inner light is eternal. It never dims or is extinguished. But a challenging emotional state might prevent one from experiencing his or her spiritual light.

Maybe what we're calling "faith" is what I'm calling spiritual strength—or at least it's one of the ingredients. Perhaps it's not all of it, but it's one of the ingredients that go into gaining spiritual strength. I've never lost faith.

TS   What is your view of the way our culture approaches depression? And do you think there is a better way for us to take care of people in pain?

SI   I was interviewed for a movie recently and asked about mental illness, my own depression, and the shamanic view of these things. There is so much stigma in our culture around the label of mental illness, about people who go through depression or who go through an experience of disintegration of the ego. In our culture, we often look at these people as outcasts instead of realizing that they are going through a deep inner process and [considering] what is needed is to hold such people in loving community. Shamanic cultures knew how to create community to hold people during these passages and to welcome them back into community life when they were ready to return. We don't know how to do that in our culture, and so people do become outcasts. We're seeing a huge number of kids in their twenties who are becoming homeless because that's where they're finding a community of people who understand them—rather than trying to change them. There needs to be a way to accept people and to create community for them while they go through dark, initiatory phases.

I knew an Ulcchi shaman from Siberia who was forty years old when I met her. She would talk to me about one of the most powerful shamans in her community, whom they called "Grandmother." She had gone through a psychotic experience for eighteen years, which served as her initiation into becoming a shaman. The community knew what was happening for her and that she would return with psychic gifts and healing abilities. They kept her in a safe place for the duration, ensuring she didn't hurt herself. After eighteen years, she emerged as a powerful healer who worked on behalf of the community.

I think that the real issue in our culture is the stigma that goes along with some of the states that people go through, our misunderstanding of the process, and then labeling these people as outcasts instead of being able to create a space to hold such a new birth of spiritual being. Ultimately, these experiences often result in a person cultivating more gifts to contribute to the community. So, while I can see my depression as a hard thing to endure, even I have to acknowledge that I've given a lot of gifts back to the world community. Those gifts have come through the states that I've undergone, the continual initiation processes of going down into the dark, having parts of my personality being annihilated, and then coming back into the world with gifts that I can share to help others. I think the real *key* is that there is no such thing as a permanent dark state without a rebirth process. Rather, everything is part of a cycle and has to be looked at as part of a cycle.

TS   You've been able to contribute so much to the world, Sandy, in so many ways. What might you say to a person who has come through the depths of depression, but hasn't seen this sort of fruit in their lives, where they have been able to give back to the world?

SI   It might not be that everybody who goes through a place of deep depression comes back to share gifts that they're aware of, but they do come back changed. Anybody who comes through a place of darkness, that place of disintegration, whether they're aware of it or not, has gone through a shamanic rite of passage. In order to come to the other side of that, whether they're conscious of it or not, they emerge as a new person more in touch with their authentic self. They come through sculpted into a new being, like somebody who's gone through a terrible divorce or has survived cancer or some other physical illness or lost their job or lost their house. Some people are very aware that they have grown, evolved, and have a deeper appreciation for life when they come through to the other side. But others might not receive that reflection from the outer world of the newness of being reborn with stronger spiritual strength and gifts they now contribute to their community.

The underlying message here is that anybody who's come through the other side of depression is changed. And that's what initiation is; it creates a shift in our life through which we come back transformed and in a different state of evolution. It just depends on how aware we are. While I can imagine somebody not being aware of it, I don't see a possibility for somebody coming back unchanged. Rather, they are in a new season of their life, in some different form than they were in before.

16

Wholehearted Expression

Mark Nepo

> Living wholeheartedly has brought me through the bottom of my pain and sadness into the well of all feeling, into the well of all spirit—to the common well where I don't just touch into my own humanity, but I touch into everyone who has ever lived.

In my life as a writer and poet, I started out like any artist: devoted to learning a craft and hoping to write one or two great poems in my life that might add to the literature. But then, a funny thing happened on the way to becoming a poet—in my mid-thirties, I was stricken with cancer. For all my want to change the world, life was changing me and I had to forget writing great poems because I needed to discover true poems that would help me live. During that difficult journey, I wrote constantly. Not because I thought the poems would make a good book, but because poetry had become the rope of expression I used every day to climb into the next day.

During those difficult days, I learned that the journey and experience of expression is at the heart of all poetry, all art. Poetry is the unexpected utterance of the soul, an act of expression that is cleansing, renewing. And living wholeheartedly has brought me through the bottom of my pain and sadness into the well of all feeling, into the well of all spirit—to the common well where I don't just touch into my own humanity, but I touch into everyone who has ever lived. Through expression, we connect with everything, we experience Oneness. It is authentic expression that moves us further in our life of transformation.

There are many passages that block our expression. Depression is one of them. For me, depression is the grip of our depth of feeling in the midst of our transformation. It is dark because we can't see our way through it, not because its nature is dark. Our vision is limited so we stumble and fall as we encounter the difficulty that comes with tumbling through periods of transformation.

While the role of expression is to be a continual catalyst for transformation, depression is a cramp in the muscle of the soul that prevents it from continuing to express. What is not *ex*pressed is *de*pressed. It's important to say that the grip of depression is no one's fault, any more than pneumonia is anyone's fault. Though pneumonia is more easily treated.

The pain of depression becomes acute when the depths of awakening—all the feeling and struggle and difficulty—get cramped or paralyzed, and we feel incompetent as we get stuck. Depression locks us in a downward spiral in which we can't access the full spectrum of human moods—whether it's through trauma, a mix of our biochemistry, relationships that are not growing, or our own memories of the way things were or ought to be. When we are stuck in one aspect of life, things can't move forward.

One way the Buddhist tradition describes the difference between pain and suffering is to say that pain is the friction that comes from the turning of the wheel of life. This friction is inevitable. Now say we're in a good place that we don't want to end, or maybe we're afraid of what's coming. So we try to stop the wheel of life from turning. We try to hold it back, to keep it from moving forward. The reality is that no one can stop the wheel of life, and when we try to halt its turning, we add stress and pain to our experience. Whether this happens consciously or unconsciously, this added pain is what the Buddhists describe as suffering.

Life continually goes up and down. People who are transcendent and romantic freeze the upside of life while nihilists, existentialists, or pessimists want to freeze the dip in the wheel of life. But the truth is that it never stays the same. It continuously moves. So part of our challenge in a life of transformation is to open our hearts to all of it, not skipping over anything, because it's the Wholeness of Life that is transforming.

Here's another way to look at the unending turn of the wheel of life. It takes six million pollen grains to seed one peony. Now, if you're one of the grains that don't grow into a flower, you can think life is terrible and dark, even evil. And if you're the one pollen grain that becomes the peony, you think, "Oh, life is such a gift, it's a miracle!"

But the larger truth is: there are a hundred ways that we blossom and a hundred ways we don't. Both processes are part of being alive, and it's only when we get stuck in halfheartedness that we begin to spiral darkly. We live in a culture where our halfheartedness wants to latch on to the high of becoming the peony and never let go: "Oh, give me sex, give me intoxication, give me fame, give me wealth, give me adventure, give me anything to stave off the thousand times I won't blossom." And likewise, we can also get stuck in the lowness when we don't blossom. Then we become inconsolable and truly heartbroken, seemingly beyond repair.

When not depressed, we can see that depression by itself is part of the weather of the soul, part of the whole range of human experience, which includes sadness, chaos, anger, doubt, and fear. But here's the rub: When depressed, the dark cloud that engulfs us prevents us from seeing and feeling the rest of the human journey. This is one reason why depression is so devastating—it mutes a person's entire existence.

Let's pause here to look at a misperception in how we've been taught to regard ourselves. For this, let's turn to the work of scholar Neil Douglas-Klotz, who has beautifully translated the words of Jesus from Aramaic, the original language it's believed Jesus spoke. Of the many things Douglas-Klotz has found, the one that touches me most is this: In the King James version of the Bible, Jesus is translated as saying, "Be Thou perfect," but in the original Aramaic, the phrase translates as, "Be Thou wholehearted." Here is a two-thousand-year-old fork in the road of education. We have been told for centuries to live without flaws, when Jesus encouraged us to be wholehearted.

The majesty of our human soul and the majesty of love are that they help us recall that we are wholehearted. By opening our heart at any time, we have the opportunity to recover our wholeheartedness. Living this way gives us a taste of Oneness that can help us outwait the storms of existence.

Nonetheless, it's an incredibly hard odyssey to outwait the cloud of depression. When I've been under dark clouds, the beginning of being able to move through that depression was realizing that all of life isn't dark simply because I'm dark. The sun doesn't stop shining because there are clouds; we just can't see or feel its rays. By their nature, clouds pass. We can have faith in that.

And if that spot of faith seems impossible to reach, antidepressants can relieve the acuteness of depression—the stuckness of depression—enough to help people start to see that there is light above and around their cloud. Then therapy and other forms of help can uncover paths toward feeling the Wholeness of Life again. Antidepressants are tools, and thank God we have them. While any tool can be misused, no one would tell me not to use crutches if I broke my leg. We'd all agree that I need the crutches for support before I can find my strength again. The beneficial use of antidepressants is to soften the acuteness of depression so that we can engage the journey, not hide from it.

Yet antidepressants are often misperceived as pills that will simply numb us out or offer a shortcut or a quick fix. But these projections mask a society that's afraid of feeling. We want to run from what is painful or even uncomfortable, and, of course, we can't. So we use an endless variety of agents to numb us to the basic, ever-changing conditions of being human. The quick fixes in our culture are more readily found in abuses of alcohol, sex, gambling, shopping, sports, or reality television.

Since the beginning of time, no one has been able to bypass the inevitable experience of both sorrow and pleasure. And everyone who's ever lived has had to face the challenge of making sense of these basic human feelings.

I recently learned something profound about our relationship to sorrow and pleasure. I was at a friend's house where I picked up a smooth, leather-bound 1903 edition of Oscar Wilde's poems. On the very page I opened was a prose poem I had never seen, written in 1894, called "The Artist."

In the poem, an artist is compelled to create a statue out of bronze that would represent "The Pleasure that Abides for a Moment." There's only one problem: When he looks around, there's no more bronze left in the world; there's no material to form his sculpture with. So he drifts about and then remembers there is one bronze statue left that he himself had carved. Years earlier, when he lost a dear friend, he fashioned a statue of "The Sorrow that Endures For Ever" to place on his friend's tomb. Now he goes to the tomb, where he relives his memories and the sorrow of his deep loss returns. He falls into a state of depression for a while, and then finally removes the statue from the tomb. He carries it and puts it in a furnace to melt it back down to raw bronze. And out of "The Sorrow that Endures For Ever" *melted down,* he fashions "The Pleasure that Abides for a Moment."

That furnace is the fire of transformation, and we are the bronze. And sooner or later, everyone alive is going to have to go through the fire to transform his or her sorrow into pleasure. It's scary, and there's no guarantee that we won't burn up in the furnace. We have no idea how long we will be in the furnace, in a depression, experiencing our soul on fire, feeling like there's no way out.

This is profound. The task is not to cheer up or to turn from our difficult feelings to happier ones. The journey of transformation is to take our sorrows and losses and wounds and disappointments and to somehow, with the love of others, melt them all down in the bottom of our being, so we can reform who we are into the peace that abides in the center of every moment. That feeling of peace is the pleasure of being that comes from being remade in the furnace of life. And no matter how briefly, the very peace we rest on is comprised of the essential elements of our journey reshaped in the fire of our days.

Still, none of this is easy. Even when remade in the furnace of life, we smolder for a long while. This is another form of depression, the aftermath of being transformed and remade by experience. When I smolder and feel depressed, I go to the ocean because its endless waves help me remember that there are a thousand feelings and that, like those waves, no two are the same. There's a rise and a fall to each; there's a crest and a dip to each. And we can ride every feeling from its dip to its next swell. Each can take us to its crest, and for the moment we can see the horizon. That's important, for it gives us a moment of pleasure. It gives us a moment of relief. Even when all we know is pain, even when we're in chronic, debilitating pain, there are moments when it lets up before it grips us again.

Hippocrates said, "Pleasure is the absence of pain." Having experienced deep pain myself, that makes a lot of sense because the instant that the pain relaxes its grip, it's not just offering relief—it's building a foundation of moments to stand on that will support me when pain or sorrow grips me next. If we have enough of these moments, we can start to feel a ground under the recurring pain, under the recurring sadness, under the recurring sorrow.

When I first received treatment for cancer, I had a tumor on my brain that led to surgery on my skull. I wasn't afraid of dying then, but terrified of what I had to go through. Then, within a year, I found another tumor quietly growing in a rib on my back. That's when I felt depressed. Not only was cancer back, but I wondered: *Did I waste a miracle? Did I waste my second chance? Did I fail in some way? What now?* I fell completely into my fear that I was going to die. When I tried the same efforts I had enlisted the first time around and none of them worked, I dropped into a depressed state. That was my first extended moment—days, weeks, months—of true depression, because I didn't know how to get out of the situation I was in.

I was left with nothing to do but surrender to being in the furnace. I had to open my heart to the time I had and to whatever was around me. It was opening to the humility, surrender, and acceptance of *this is where I am* that made the difference. Through that opening, I gave myself over and asked for help. I surrendered to whatever help I could get, because I no longer had the option to be discerning about my treatment. In desperation, I said, "I don't want to die yet. Help me. Somebody, anybody." Having preferences became irrelevant. Like when the ambulance arrives, you don't check the paramedic's driver's license. Instead you say, "Thank you. I'm in your hands." On the other side of that fire, I found myself raw and vulnerable. I was still here, but not the same person who entered the fire. Slowly, I had to discover who I was again.

Another profound example of moving through the fire is Dante's *Divine Comedy*, which portrays the journey during midlife as we climb from hell through purgatory to paradise. It's tempting to make a mental cartoon of that image and think we're climbing out of the darkness into the light so we can end up standing on some shining hill. But Jungian analyst Helen Luke describes the journey in a way that's much more true to life. When we consider the realms that Dante passes through to be states of consciousness, we can appreciate them as a map of the inner journey through life. She describes hell as the cost of false living, purgatory as the struggle to be real, and paradise as the struggle to *stay* real. Notice we are never far from struggle.

But the story I want to tell happens in the middle of the *Divine Comedy*. You see, right smack in the middle of this three-hundred-page epic poem, there's a wall of fire.

When Dante arrives at this wall of fire, he's afraid. He doesn't think he can go any farther, for he's certain he can't go through such a wall. To this point on his journey, Dante has been accompanied by the spirit guide Virgil, who turns to him and says, "It is the fire that will burn, but it won't consume. Yes, you'll be burned and you'll be hurt, but you will be okay. It won't consume you—instead it will transform you." Dante listens, but continues to refuse. Virgil insists, saying, "I know you can do it. Not only *can* you do it, you really *have* to do it, or you're not going to grow. I will be there on the other side when you get through."

Virgil walks away, and Dante summons his courage and goes through the wall of fire. While he's somewhat burned—nicked and cut—he emerges okay. Quite simply, he is overjoyed to have gotten through this transformative fire, which turns out to mark the final passage out of purgatory. From this point, he is closer to paradise than to hell.

Next, something interesting happens that I find very revealing about the journey we all must make—it speaks to the loneliness we experience, both in depression and in moments of deep clarity. While Dante is relieved to be on the other side of the wall of fire, he looks for Virgil. But the angel who has guided him through so much has disappeared, and is neither seen nor mentioned for the entire second half of the journey. Now, we could conclude that Virgil betrayed Dante: what kind of teacher just disappears? But if we go deeper, it's clear that once we move through the fire of transformation, we become our own guide.

The challenge in traveling through this life together is that we can't spare each other from having to go through the wall of fire. If I fall down out here in the world, you can help me up. If you're hungry, I can give you food. But when we're each facing our own inner journey, then if you fall down, I can't pick you up, and you can't give me the inner food I need. So we're left to be in heartfelt, wholehearted company with each other.

Toward the end of his life, Ivan Illich—a sociologist from the 1960s—coined the term *spiritual hospitality* and defined it as "helping another cross a threshold." I love this because the definition doesn't say what threshold. Spiritual hospitality doesn't mean we tell another person how to make the journey. It doesn't mean we tell another person whether it's a good or bad decision he or she is making—just that we help him or her cross a threshold.

No one can go through the fire for us, and yet, no one can make it alone. If I'm your Virgil, I can try to give you water while you're in the fire of transformation. I can try to keep you company, but it's not my fire, so I won't get burned the same way you will. The real courage of compassion is keeping each other company, honestly and deeply. While we can love each other and walk together, no one can turn another's sorrow into pleasure. We can only *companion each other* with that blessed kind of spiritual friendship that lets us know we can make it through the fire.

But there's a paradox here that I've discovered the more I've grown. I have many friends and relationships that are important to me—I'm not solitary or alone. And still, on the deepest level, as I grow in wonder and in connection to the Unity of Life, there's a certain loneliness that comes with that depth. The most revealing moments I have of being alive are when I'm alone, when I am my own guide.

I was recently in New York City, eating alone at an old café in Hell's Kitchen. My table was set against a brick wall, and a little oil lamp was burning on the table. While I ate cheese and wine, all these feelings flooded through me and I experienced a sense of heartbreak, loss, and sadness. There was a little flicker in the oil lamp that wavered as the small light hit the brick wall. In my aloneness, that little patch of light on an old brick wall revealed eternity. In that moment, it was the light that has flickered on all the brick walls where people have rested their heads forever, tired of their losses. And it didn't make me feel small or lonely; it made me feel like I was a voice in that chorus. It made me feel like, "Yes, the only thing I can do is feel my loss. I'm not alone in that." Because everyone who's ever lived has had to feel it, to lean their head somewhere against a brick wall while there's a flicker of light nearby that they may or may not see.

Here is the poem that came from that moment:

BETWEEN THE WALL AND THE FLAME
You ask, "How can you believe in
anything when there's pain everywhere?"
And I see the pain in your face. I have no
answer, anymore than day can make its case
in the middle of the night. Yes, things are
breaking constantly and people, bent from
their nature, are cruel and our desperation
leads us to an excess that is even too heavy
for the planet to bear. Yet, I am in a wine
bar in Hell's Kitchen, against a brick wall,
and the small flame from the oil lamp is
letting the wall whisper its long history.
And somehow in the lighted inch of
brick, what matters flickers and I feel
everything. Something between the wall
and the flame flutters like a butterfly
carrying the secret of peace, unseen,
unnoticed. And even seeing it, and
feeling it briefly, I don't know how to
speak of it. It's as if under the earthquake

of existence, an infinite hand holds the
ball of fire that is our world. Now someone nearby pokes me and asks, "So, are
you talking about God?" This is beyond
anything I have a concept for. We're like
small urchins churned over in the surf of
time. There's so much more than we can
know. But you are still hurting. So I'll
stop talking. Come, put your head
on my shoulder.

The reward for expressing a moment like this is that doing so constantly renews us with the life force that is coursing through the bodies
and souls of everyone who's ever lived and ever will live. Entering
such moments is how we express ourselves into being. This expression doesn't have to be poetry, as the ongoing conversation you have
with yourself, written or not, skilled or not, *is* expression. It doesn't
even have to be verbal. Meditative traditions are streams of wordless
expression that connect the individual to the Living Universe and, as
such, renew our aliveness. Expression doesn't take away our experience,
and it can't take away our pain, but it can offer us context. When I'm
experiencing pain or sadness or fear, my sense of things enlarges by
expressing whatever I'm going through. And when I enlarge my sense
of things, it returns me to the stream of life.

I once experienced a profound artistic depression. My second book
was an epic poem called *Fire Without Witness.* It took me ten years to
write and was the deepest dive into the unconscious I have ever made.
It had been accepted for publication while I was in the hospital with
cancer. So while I was thrilled, publishing it didn't turn out to be as
important as I had thought. Four or five years after it was published, I
discovered, quite by accident, that the publisher hadn't made an effort
to find me before destroying fifteen hundred copies of the book. The
destruction of something I had labored and loved into being devastated
me. It led me into deep, dark inquiries about our impermanence, like,
"What am I doing this for? My words can't even survive or be seen

now, let alone a hundred years from now." I was very sullen and darkly wondering, "Why bother? What's the point?" This went on for months.

Then I went to New Mexico to visit a friend. I was driving from Albuquerque to Santa Fe, admiring the beautiful mountains, when suddenly the sunlight came from behind a cloud and illuminated those mountains. It was as if the mountains were talking to me, to my depression, and their presence said, "We have suffered all the names you can throw on us. We have Native American names, we have Spanish names, we have European names, and we have outlived them all to receive this light on our faces for the billionth time." And suddenly, I saw that if those mountains could endure the indignities of time, I could endure my book being destroyed. It wasn't like a switch had gone on, but more like I had come out from under my cloud. I stepped through the cloud and began to find a path beyond it. There is a kinship of being in that story: everything is alive with expression, everything a singular gift, including a mountain range.

Having said that, I also want to confirm that while life is full, there is also an emptiness that is opened by the sheer authenticity of living—a spaciousness through which we can relate to the depth of what it is to be here, to be alive. Consider that almost all musical instruments are hollowed out in order to make music: string instruments, wind instruments, percussion instruments. Without that space, that emptiness, music can't be heard. But we're so preoccupied and fearful of emptiness that we're taught to run from it—toward whatever can take us out of the emptiness. We live in such a fill-'er-up society because we're afraid of the emptiness and even of the reverberation of the music that happens in that emptiness.

Yet I'm starting to understand that we're given both a gift and an emptiness so we can develop a relationship between the two. When life digs a hole in us, that hurts. And while it's a very natural reflex to shovel earth back into the hole, life excavates our depths so that we can make our music. If we become devoted miners with headlamps on, we can see what is revealed in those depths.

This prose poem tries to bring to the surface the relationship between our light and our depth:

THE GIFT AND THE EMPTINESS

We are each born with a gift and an emptiness, and
given a life to be in conversation with them, to have one
fill the other. It doesn't matter where the emptiness is in
our life or what the gift is, it is always the journey of a
life on Earth to discover how they meet and complete
each other. We waste so much time trying to hide our
emptiness, feel ashamed of our emptiness, eliminate our
emptiness, feel victimized because we have an emptiness,
or feel we are entitled not to have any emptiness, that
we are diverted from our soul's journey. This diversion
gives rise to the blame game and keeps us from
inhabiting the depths opened by the emptiness that
can only be illumined by the light of our gift.

Our personal emptiness is uncovered through our sense of lack, of
loss, of being unearthed, but I have found that when I can get to
the bottom of my personal emptiness, I open up into a Universal
Emptiness—and there, I begin to feel the bareness of being, the
spaciousness of existence. The Grand Canyon is among the greatest
natural emptinesses we know on Earth. People save money and go on
vacation to stand at its rim. Why? Because somehow, just being close
to that vastness invokes feelings of eternity. We see life beyond our
own life, we feel the mystery.

It's similar with our personal love. If I can go to the bottom of
my personal love, for any one thing or being or object, I open into
a Universal Love that's not attached to any one thing or place. In the
last year, I witnessed my ninety-three-year-old father's slow avalanche
toward death. And in the last few months, our beloved dog died.
Those have been incredibly sad losses. I'm certainly in a state of somber
heartache, but I don't think I'm depressed, at least not so far, and here's
why: because the other periods of deep sorrow I've been through have
enabled me to experience more acceptance this time around. I feel that
life is holding these losses with me. So I'm sad but at peace this time.

This poem was written from inside the emptiness of my grief:

THE ANGEL OF GRIEF

Does the tree at that knot twenty
feet up feel its missing rib, the way
I feel you gone these long years? Loss
plays us like a violin, never free of its rub.
It simply lessens its intensity till only the
one closest to what was lost can hear it.
If you haven't lost something or someone,
this will seem sad, even frightening. But
after a century of heart-time, I went to
the immortals who envy us our ability
to feel and forget. They looked at me
with their longing to be human. And
the saddest among them took my hand
and said, "I would give eternity to live with
what you're given, and to feel what is
opened by what is taken away."

When I go to the bottom of my love for the beings I have lost, I recognize why sages and saints can run around loving people and places and things without needing causes to love. Touching on the bareness of being directly, they don't need reasons to love. And likewise, they don't need the trigger of loss or pain to open them to the Universal Emptiness. They break through to the shimmer of being here just by being alive.

As I've grown older, I feel life is asking me to practice being a very particular person in my particular life here on Earth without losing sight of, or ceasing to feel, the incredible mysterious Whole of which I'm a part. So while I experience great loss in my life—for example, feeling how devastated I am right now by the loss of our beloved dog, Mira, who graced our lives for thirteen and a half years—I don't minimize it. And yet, I try to stay open to the ever-changing life force that exists in my grief and beyond my grief, that exists everywhere and has for eternity—not as an abstract idea, but as a Living Wholeness of which I'm a part and our dog was a part and you're a part and we're all a part. When I can feel both—my particular life in the swell of all life—I feel at peace; I feel an acceptance in being part of this unending, unimaginable life force.

During my times of depression, I couldn't make this journey from my personal emptiness to the Universal Emptiness. It's a big question we each need to ask ourselves: how do we move from the pain of our personal emptiness to the universal bareness of being and the peace and acceptance it can offer? If we knew the answer, then no one would go through the inevitable journey of being human. And if we could choose, we wouldn't go through a life of transformation, because it's such a long and hard journey.

But it helps me when I'm depressed to remember that there *is* a universal spaciousness and bareness of being, even though I can't find it. And life relentlessly asks me to open my heart even more—even though I'm overcome with pain and grief. However, we're not being asked to open our heart only to the pain and grief, but to *widen* our heart to include those things and everything else. Because we don't know what will enter our experience and restore us.

When I can feel what is mine to feel *and* widen my heart to let in the rest of life, the quest changes. It becomes, "How can I feel everything that's not hurting as much as what hurts and let the two things mix?" That's what starts to rearrange what's going on in me. That's what starts a conversation again between resilience and wholeheartedness. Try as we will, we can't extract the peace from the pain. In fact, I believe that peace is not the endpoint of stillness after we've gotten through our difficulties—rather it is the ocean of being that holds all difficulty.

The oldest tools we've been given to reawaken our resilience are holding and listening. And I can say that holding and listening have never let me down. When I don't know what to think or where to go or what to do, I try to open my heart and hold myself, or another, or life, or the truth. Then I can put down my assumptions and conclusions. Then the prayer is just listening to how things are, not asking for things to be different. When we can hold and listen to who we are and what's around us, a little light can come through and start to dissolve the cloud that engulfs us.

After all these years, I have to say that more than manipulating words, being a poet is trying to bear witness to how things are, to how all things are connected. Being an awakened spirit is trying to keep each other company as we move through the furnace, through the incarnation of being here, through the friction of what it is to be alive.

After all these years, I'm left in the open as a poet who wants to *be* the poem, and the words are merely my trail. Still, I struggle to get up every day and dare to be expressive. When I can, my heart tends to open and my being begins to show itself in the world. And sometimes, when feeling the particulars of *this* life and the particulars of *all* lives, I feel a sense of acceptance and peace. Sometimes, with the help of others, I can connect beyond my brokenness to everything else that is not broken. This brings me tenderly into the bareness of being that has always been. If we can widen our hearts, we can meet each other there.

17

Letting Depression Come

Sally Kempton

I really thought I'd processed my shadow issues.
I'd gone through intense kundalini-inspired
purification. I'd lived with two hard-core gurus.
Moreover, I'd done years of practices designed to
purify my mind—everything from eighteen-hour
japa sessions to ten-day juice fasts to hours spent
mentally throwing my karmic patterns into an
inner fire. I'd even done targeted psychotherapy.
The one thing I had never done was to sit with my
most negative feelings in a spirit of inquiry and
with the intention to let it all come out.

I grew up in a family that skewed toward depression—the mild, melancholic, weltschmerz-y sort of depression, leavened by jokes, but essentially bleak. By the time I was twelve, I was consciously invoking sad feelings. When I conjured up a sad image, and stayed with the feelings, I'd get a pleasurable softness in my heart and sometimes tears. Tears that felt sweet, even strangely healing. So I spent whole afternoons immersed in songs of unrequited love—English folk ballads, Frank Sinatra's *In the Wee Small Hours* album, country songs—whatever I could find that reliably made me cry. Melancholy, I believed, was a sign of depth. Didn't the romantic poets feel sad most of the time? Didn't William James, van Gogh, Holden Caulfield, and pretty much everyone with whom I identified? I could list a raft of melancholic geniuses whose lives *proved* the link between depression and artistic talent. "Despair is mine," I wrote at seventeen, savoring the juicy depths of it: "my dear companion."

Then, in my late twenties, I fell into a real, chemical depression, and that was when I stopped romanticizing despair. The darkness came on at the end of a three-month spiritual training. I'd entered the training with the idea that by the time I was finished, I'd be enlightened, or at least in a better state than I'd been before. Instead, I got a hard look at the reality behind my self-image. The first real peek into the fragility of the false self's structure is never pretty. But I was dealing with it, until we entered a two-week group retreat.

MY FIRST DESCENT

It was my first silent retreat. The program included a special diet, long hours of meditation, and no talking at all. Halfway through the retreat, I began to feel profoundly lonely and scared, and within a couple of days the sense of isolation and fear morphed into a dense grey fog. A glass wall separated me from the rest of the world. I couldn't read, because every book I picked up seemed to describe a different permutation of human suffering that overwhelmed me.

After the retreat ended and I returned home, I found a little relief from Woody Allen movies, and more relief from the soothingly repetitious words of the Sanskrit mantra that I was working with. I grasped at mantra. Its resonant sounds, which I could glom on to mentally, offered me an alternative to thinking and an escape from the endless cascade of self-loathing thoughts that cycled through my mind and froze my heart.

Normal conversation was an exercise in alienation. To be around friends was torture, because their casual enjoyment of life—and their kindly attempts to cheer me up—threw my pain into high gear. Anne Sexton described this state when she wrote:

> Now listen, life is lovely, but I Can't Live It. To be alive,
> yes—but not to be able to live it. Ay, that's the rub. I am
> like a stone that lives, locked outside of all that's real. I
> wish, or think I wish, that I were dying of something,

for then I could be brave, but not to be dying and yet
. . . and yet to [be] behind a wall, watching everyone
talk behind a gray foggy wall, to live but . . . to do it all
wrong . . . I'm not a part. I'm not a member. I'm frozen.

That was me.

Then, after three months of mental agony, the cloud gradually
lifted. At the time, the shift felt miraculous and spontaneous. Looking
back, with the knowledge we've derived from neuroscience, I would
guess that this sudden resolution may have been the result of developing a new set of neurological pathways, partly as a result of the intense
mantra practice I did.

But my miraculous "cure" left in its wake a conviction that my old
way of living was an invitation to depression, and that the only path
forward was to throw myself into spiritual practice and never look
back. Practice had been the closest thing to a lifeline during the dark
months, and I took that lesson seriously. In the years that followed,
the story I told myself about the dark period was that it had been my
personal wake-up call. In more grandiose moments, I likened it to the
Buddha's recognition of the inevitability of suffering, or Prince Rama's
powerful statement in the beginning of Yoga Vashistha:

When I consider the pitiful fate of living beings, fallen
into the dreadful pit of sorrow, I am filled with grief. I
am confused. I shudder, and at every step I am afraid . . .
obviously this world is full of pain and death; how does it
become a source of joy, without befuddling one's heart?

That, I believed, is the real use of despair. If it gets bad enough, it will
turn you toward dispassion, detachment, and radical inner practice.

NEVER AGAIN?

Wake-up call or not, I was determined never to experience that darkness again. For the next fifteen years, I kept myself rigorously on the

light side. I had a whole backpack of state-shifting methods. Feeling sad? Intensify my mantra practice. Dark mood? Take a fast walk. Anxiety? Yoga worked. Hurt feelings? Throw myself into work, or tune in to the presence of the aware witness behind thoughts and emotions. I did everything I could to distance myself from people who brought me down—especially my own family. And, for a few of those years, I lost all empathy for unhappiness. Once, a friend suffering from prolonged chemical depression told me that he was checking himself into an institution because he could no longer handle his inner pain. I gave him a pep talk, suggesting that he pull up his socks and intensify his practice.

"You're a brilliant poet and serious practitioner," I told him. "And anyway, you know better. You know you're not your thoughts or feelings—you're the knower of them!" He didn't argue with me. He just rolled his eyes. He checked himself into McLean Hospital two weeks later, and I congratulated myself for knowing the secret of staying in the light.

At the time, I didn't realize that it's impossible to outrun your own darkness forever. In fact, I was well into my forties before the darkness caught up with me again. Even then, it took a couple of years to surrender to the fact that I wasn't going to be able to step into real freedom without learning how to walk through the thickets of my own depression, anger, jealousy, and the rest of the gremlins lurking in the corners of my heart.

But by that time, I actually had an inner ground to stand on. Over the years, meditation had taught me how to shift my attention from the surface of my awareness to the subtle witnessing Awareness from which thoughts and emotions emerge. As the felt sense of that Awareness became more rooted, so did a feeling of confidence, a trust in my own ground. I don't believe that anyone should try to face up to naked despair without having developed a rock-steady relationship to that inner Witness, the loving Presence behind thoughts.

Without knowing that aware Presence, I never would have been able to look at myself without shrinking back. The sense of myself as Awareness was not only a bulwark, but it also let me discern the difference between a useful, workable, and potentially life-transforming depression and the darkness that can rob your life of all meaning and even the energy to change.

LOOKING AT THE FLAVORS OF MY DEPRESSION

As I developed a sense of Presence and became able to look at my experience, one thing I saw was that just as there are different kinds of love, there are different kinds of depression. There's depression as a mood, a pervasive feeling of life as a glass half empty. There's the depression that comes with loss, but lifts when your life takes a new turn. There's the basic seasonal-affective-disorder type of depression, familiar to anyone who has had to live through a long, dark winter. And there's the depression that comes over you when your life is stagnating, which I learned to recognize as a kind of calling to step into the unknown.

But these are all different from the sheer, unremitting misery of a genuine biochemical depression. I know very few people who've experienced a long-term clinical downer as workable, or even endurable, without some kind of temporary chemical intervention. I've known more than one practitioner who tried to meditate their way out of a biochemical depression, and then found that when they finally surrendered to taking a little Prozac or Zoloft, not only did their mood lift, but their practice soared as well.

So, I've come to believe that practicing with depression starts with knowing which kind of depression you're dealing with, and thus what kind of intervention helps it become workable. Unlike the biochemical depressions, a useful depression is often a disguised wake-up call, designed to nudge you toward some sort of transformation. Workable depression is often situational. It signals you that it's time to do something about your marriage, your job, or the fact that you've let go of your creativity. Some forms of situational depression begin to lift the moment you take action to make changes. Others demand that you grieve a loss, make peace with a health crisis, or take time for rest and healing. Depressions like this teach you. They're part of nearly everyone's journey.

For me, the untangling of this particular depression came in layers. The first layer was definitely situational, triggered by a living situation that left me feeling powerless and creatively unstrung. That phase began with a dream of slogging through mud and moved into an intense confrontation with my buried anger and feelings of rebellion. And then, the grief came.

I mourned the risks I hadn't taken, the adventures I'd backed away from. I squirmed in shame for everyone I'd hurt. And I took some life-shifting actions. I moved out of the spiritual community I'd been living in and started rethinking my approach to practice. All this took a few years—but turned out to be merely a warm-up for the self-confrontation that marked my true encounter with depression.

GETTING NAKED WITH MYSELF

Since the inner journey is usually a spiral rather than a straight line, I should have known that I'd have to revisit the feelings that had knocked me on my butt in my twenties. But truthfully, I was surprised that they were still there. I really thought I'd processed my shadow issues. I'd gone through several bouts of fairly intense kundalini-inspired purification. I'd lived with two hard-core gurus, neither of whom was shy about pointing out my shortcomings. Moreover, I'd done years of practices designed to purify my mind—everything from eighteen-hour *japa* sessions to ten-day juice fasts to hours spent mentally throwing my karmic patterns into an inner fire. I'd even done some targeted psychotherapy.

The one thing I had never done was to sit with my most negative feelings in a spirit of inquiry and with the intention to let it all come out. So, perhaps it shouldn't have been surprising that even after thirty years of practice, unprocessed layers of resentment, grief, and basic self-loathing were still hiding in the basement of my psyche, controlling my moods and tainting my practice with escapism. As any good Jungian knows, there is no magic bullet for dissolving those layers, any more than there is a pill you can take to dissolve your self-contraction. But there does come a moment when you're ready to have those layers come out and look you in the face. In my experience, most of us can't do this until we've developed a real connection to the Inner Self, or Presence, or Awareness, or the Witness I described earlier. Without that, staring hard into the inner darkness becomes unbearable and debilitating—especially when you have issues with self-loathing and fear. In my early days as a practitioner, I could have no more stood in the fire of my own psychic debris than I could have composed a Bach cantata. Without the ability to experience love and awareness as your true self, staring hard at the inner darkness is unbearable.

And, by the way, I didn't actually make a decision to face into depression. It simply swam up one evening, accompanied by its friends: self-loathing, shame, and resentment. As always, it took over my consciousness—those old neural pathways (or *samskaras,* as yogis call them) had never really gone away, only gotten somewhat attenuated. But to my everlasting gratitude, there was another, parallel pathway, a steady thread of Awareness that, when I paid attention to it, would expand to hold the feelings without completely giving in to them. Somehow, Awareness knew that there was no need to deny these feelings and thoughts, or even to figure out some intervention to make them go away. Awareness just sat with them.

Several times a week, for nearly six months, I would find myself lying on my couch, watching layers of my unconscious self-rejection, resentment, and despair rise, take me over, and dissolve. I danced with anger. I writhed with shame. I stared into the self-justifications, the excuses. I sank through the layers of despondency. Yes, when it got really uncomfortable, I'd take refuge in a novel or a Netflix video. But mostly, I let it come.

For the first time, I understood what it is really all about. It's all about letting it come, and letting it go, and remembering to be the Awareness that holds it. Sometimes I'd remind myself, "It's all made of particles of mind-stuff," or "All thoughts are empty." But mostly I just let it be.

Over time, I learned to ask questions of my feelings:

- What should I let go of?
- What needs to be looked at, or fixed?
- Is this old stuff, or is there something I need to change?

And often my feelings would give me practical advice:

- Take a walk.
- Call a friend.
- Try some positive self-talk.
- Stop procrastinating and sit for meditation.
- Take a bath.
- Eat something.
- Write about it.
- Start the project you've been scared of starting.

I learned to identify the feelings that were not really "mine," but belonged to my genetic heritage, or even to humanity itself. Certain skews on the world I could recognize as holdovers from my parents' worldview. Others—the sense of let-down after completing a project, for example—felt like natural contractions that are part of the flow of life energy. And there was also what I learned to think of as the sadness that melts the barriers around the heart—the empathic grieving that comes from recognizing the essential poignancy of human life.

As I learned to inquire into sad feelings, I discovered a practice that I've worked with (and taught) ever since. It looks like this:

- Recognize the feeling of sadness.
- Let go of the ideas and thoughts around it.
- Look for where the feeling is sitting in the body.
- Investigate the felt sense of it—its texture, its shape, the thoughts that accompany it.
- Imagine a space around the feeling in the body, and even around the whole body. Let this "space" surround you.
- And then sit, holding the sad energy and the space together.
- Let it all be there, without trying to change it, explain it, or make it go away.
- Keep noticing and letting go of the thoughts.

- Notice that the "space" you've imagined is full of awareness and presence—that it's a textured, kindly observer. Notice that it can interpenetrate the feelings of sadness, and that as it does, they morph.
- Gradually allow yourself to relax into the space of awareness. Notice that the energy of sadness melts into the spaciousness.

When I worked with this process, there would be times when the sad feelings would dissolve. Sometimes they wouldn't. But one thing it always did was shift, change, morph. And every time I saw this happen, I felt myself a little less identified with my own sadness, my anger, my self-criticism, a little more identified with Awareness itself.

As the months went on, and I kept sitting with those feelings, they kept showing me over and over that my emotions are not me. Dark emotions have messages. They are part of life, and sometimes they are an appropriate reaction to what's going on in the world. But they do not tell you who and what you are.

Facing into your emotional swampland reveals that all the swamp creatures are conditional. As you investigate them with the eye of Presence, you see how they constantly evanesce, how they are constantly becoming something else, and finally becoming nothing at all. And in those moments, you have the startling, exhilarating recognition that you are, actually, free. In the midst of it all, you are free.

18

The Maturing of the Soul

An Interview with Thomas Moore, PhD

> Depression allows us an entry into imagination that
> no other mood can give us. In this way it is essential.
> These experiences scoop you out and make you a
> deeper person. They may be painful experiences
> and they don't seem to be aimed at your personal
> growth, but nevertheless, they make you a deeper,
> more thoughtful, and more reflective person.

Tami Simon   What is your response to the idea that we need to
redefine depression?

Thomas Moore   Several years ago, I wrote a book titled *Dark Nights
of the Soul,* in which I specifically avoided using the word *depression.*
I wanted to address this difficult experience in a way that was less
clinical and less generic. We have so many experiences that we throw
into the bin of depression, but they're each individual and need to be
addressed specifically. For example, someone might feel depressed in
relationship to their creativity or because of loss or for no clear reason
at all. I don't know if we'd ever come to the end of a list that describes
the specific ways we experience what people call "depression." So, one
way I would like to redefine depression is by encouraging people to
be very specific about their actual experience and to come up with
descriptive names for each particular way we get depressed.

The abstract word *depression* is a heavy, Latin word that people tend
to associate with medical treatment. But if you say, "I am feeling the

loss of my youth, and I don't really know what to do about it," there is no obvious pill for that. Getting into the specifics helps us see the meaning in our experience, moving us away from medical treatment and toward the work of the soul.

TS   In your book *Care of the Soul,* you introduce something you call "the economy of the soul," and I am curious about how our experiences of the dark night might fit into that.

TM   When I use the word *economy,* I point to the various experiences that go on deeply within us and their different values. If we are in a moment of great joy and pleasure in life, it has a certain value: it's something we think is very important so we treasure it. Then we have moments of depression, and that's a different aspect of economy. We even use the word *depression* in our social economy, referring to when we go through an economic downturn. It's a word that usually describes a temporary condition, in which we don't have all the benefits, happiness, and positive outlook that we would like to have. But it does still fit within the overall economy. And just as it is in a social economy, in the economy of the soul, depressions come along in cycles. Depression also has a role to play and tends to be cyclic, so that it doesn't last forever—even though, when we're in it, we feel like it does.

TS   How does depression play a role in the economy of the soul?

TM   My friend James Hillman used to say that when we are depressed, there are places we go in the imagination that we can't go at any other time. One of the key ideas I learned from him was that the mood of depression allows us to imagine life in a certain way, which, while painful and not positive, is tremendously valuable. During times of depression, we tend to reflect on the meaning of our lives and realize that there are some things we do that don't really feed us. So, as we try to make sense of our depression, we come to discover ways that we've been living unconsciously. In those moments, we can reflect in a deeper way, asking, "What is going on?" and "Why are certain things happening?" These kinds of questions help us to sort out what actually is happening and give us an opportunity to make changes for the better. If we didn't get depressed, we wouldn't be able to ask these questions or even be aware that we have them.

TS   There seems to be a bias in Western culture toward positivity. Perhaps this is part of the reason why we feel so confused about depression and is maybe even why we see so much depression in our society.

TM   I think that Americans especially value this positive outlook. When Europeans visit America, they're surprised at how often people are smiling and giving the appearance of happiness—as if they're overdoing it. There is a style in America to value cheerfulness even if it's not real. Foreigners are surprised at the little smiley faces drawn on notes, and they think, "These people are really obsessed with being happy." When Americans go to other countries, they may feel that the people there are depressed because they don't have that same cheeriness. I work quite often in England, Scotland, and Ireland. There the level of "spiritedness," for lack of a better word, is a little bit lower than it is in America. The people there seem to both tolerate and identify more easily with a lower tone, a little darker tone to life. So yes, I do think a bias toward positivity is part of our problem. It could be a type of cover-up, because there are so many Americans who are clinically depressed. Perhaps part of the solution is to carry over some of that dark tone into everyday life and see the value in it.

Personally, when I'm in a situation where people are highly spirited and just too hilarious, it can be too much. I mean, obviously there are times when you want to enjoy yourself and just be really happy, but when it feels artificial I feel compelled to be a little darker myself rather than get too caught up in the overjoy. When I return to America from other countries, especially if I've been abroad for a few weeks, I don't want to fit in too much. I prefer a way of life in which you are free to be sad, to feel not quite so up and spirited, and even to let your depression show.

TS   Can you say more about what it means to allow yourself to have "darker tones," and how that actually looks for you?

TM   If someone asks me, "How are things going?" I may say, "Well, do you really want to know?" If they say yes, I won't try to be cheerful if I'm not feeling cheerful. Most things are mixed good and bad, so I try to express both. It feels more real that way. The depression gives a border of reality to what's going on, and I prefer that. I prefer that feeling to having to keep the spirit high all the time.

TS   In your book *Care of the Soul,* there is a section in which you write about the gift of depression as "a visit with Saturn." What do you mean by that?

TM   The idea is derived from my studies in Renaissance religion and psychology. Renaissance psychology was the focus of my doctoral dissertation and, unlike the psychology of today, its proponents focused on imagery and myth and the life of the soul. So instead of saying that someone is depressed, they would say, "This person is in Saturn." In the astrological system, Saturn is the planet that for centuries has been understood as a very valuable spirit, but one that is "heavy leaded," as lead was the metal associated with Saturn. We might say today that Saturn is heavy and depressed, but sources from a thousand years ago would say that Saturn has important things to offer as well.

One important gift was that Saturn can "give you age." Saturn is often depicted as an old man—a difficult one because you have to carry his weight and along the way he gives you age. He helps you get older. All of us, at times, tend to get stuck at a certain point in our development, and we don't age very well in the soul. We may be aging physically, but we're not necessarily getting older in soul: becoming wiser, more experienced, and carrying that kind of age with us. Especially in a culture that does not consider age desirable, people do not want to show their years internally or externally. Saturn can help with this.

I believe that in the same way, what we call depression can help us age as we feel heavy emotions, including loss, the passage of time, and hopes not lived out. Those feelings may be painful, but they're very important because they give us a sense of being wise and experienced, of having been on this earth for a while and knowing how things work. That's a gift of depression: aging with gravitas and wisdom.

TS   What do you think would have to shift in our current culture for us to be able to honor this Saturnian process?

TM   We would have to take our lives more seriously and reflect more deeply about what's going on. There has been a development in our culture toward less and less reflection. One way this has happened is through the disappearance of in-depth, reflective reporting and informed editorial refinement in newspapers and magazines. There's so much online chatter in which people express their opinions or gut feelings—and that's it. This makes us more and more susceptible to Saturnian heaviness, because it's actually more Saturnian energies that we need.

Here is a key idea that we need to understand, as a culture, in order to shift our approach to depression: *Depression is a sign of what we need.* Depression is not just an emotion or something that's happening to us that we need to get rid of or just get through—it's actually something that we need. In archetypal psychology, symptoms tell us what is missing, what is needed, and what we must pay attention to. We can view the symptoms of depression as red flags that are saying, "You're depressed. Here, this is what you need: you need to be more serious about your life; you need some heaviness, some gravitas, some weight. Let's hope that if you can honor this symptom, you can make the change. Then you don't have to experience the symptom your whole life."

TS   Have you gone through periods of depression yourself? If so, what did you learn from those experiences?

TM   Yes. I have felt that I was born with a type of depression, with Saturn prominent in my makeup—but not in a heavy, big way. I often talk about my depression as being a gray depression and not a dark, black depression. All my life I've had a low emotional level, and while I can have good times and really enjoy being together with people, at the same time I think I've always had this constant presence of Saturn. But it hasn't interfered with my life. It's not a deep depression, so I don't take medication. Still, it is there.

I haven't had many deep periods of depression in my life, but some years ago I began to feel that my life work was ending. I'd get notes from people who were wondering whether I was still alive. I was receiving fewer invitations to speak, as if the world had forgotten about me and my work. This was a depressing time for me, when I found myself thinking, "Well, maybe now I have to change my way of living and adapt to this ending." As a therapist and in my own life, my way has always been to try to go with these things as they come along, to try to be with these various moods and emotions when they come, and to just stay with them. I don't solve what is going on, but I stay with it. I really felt this ending, there's no question about that. I talked to people about it, and I didn't know how long it would last. I assumed it would last forever, actually, because I couldn't imagine it changing. The depression lasted maybe four or five years, and then it disappeared. It did change, and now I'm in a whole different place altogether.

TS   What exactly do you mean by "staying with" or "going with" your depression?

TM   I didn't get too upset about it. I accepted and embraced it as part of life. Through this experience, I suddenly had more empathy for others I know who have had similar experiences. My life was changing: I would have to adapt to a different lifestyle, and I was willing to do that. Although it wasn't easy, as time went on I realized more and more that this is just going to be the way life is. I didn't try to fight it or try to make up for it. I went with it. I certainly didn't make any effort to get out there in the world more, or do anything to try to make it different. I went with the mood of it and let the activity slow down to almost nothing, and I went inward.

In my book *Dark Nights of the Soul,* I suggest that in depression we turn to art—both paying attention to it and getting into our own art, whatever that might be. During this time, I wrote a great deal of fiction, which I love but have never published. I wrote three novels and a play during that time, which was very satisfying. Now that I'm not in that period anymore, I find myself missing the writing that I was able to do when there was nothing happening in my life.

TS   Would you say during that period there was some type of inner reflection on Saturn's gift of weight and density?

TM   Oh, yes. It certainly helped me enter my own age. It was definitely related to feeling older and beginning to relate to people differently. Because I realized that, up to that point, I hadn't taken on my age. It made quite a difference to do so. Recently, I gave a talk at a small college in Vermont and spent the day with young people in their early twenties. They were listening to me talk, and I sat in on their classes. I brought my age with me, and I talked to them about being an older person and relating to them as younger people and how important that is for people of all ages. I don't know if I could have done that if I hadn't reconciled with my aging during that time of depression.

TS   You mentioned that there's a kind of gray energy, if you will, that has always been with you, for your whole life. Can you say more about what that feels like?

TM   There's a constant part of me with a heaviness that seems to be part of my character. I try to just let that be and do what I can. Sometimes I meet others who also have that kind of innate heaviness. I was at a party a couple of years ago where there were a lot of authors who were all being very spirited and laughing and talking and having a great time. And this man, who's a quite well-known author, came over to me and said, "You look like me, not quite at home in all of this. Why don't we go over there to the side and have a talk?" We ended up talking for hours, finding in one another that we both carry this thing, this heavier outlook—which isn't at all a clinical depression. We could enjoy talking from our heaviness and find real pleasure in it, rather than being uncomfortable in that more lighthearted place.

TS   Do you believe there is a connection between the willingness to stay with the gray energy, to move through these cyclical depressions, and creative expression in art?

TM   It has been said that artists are born under Saturn, that artists discover their creative abilities through their Saturnian natures. So in this sense, Saturn may be the most important spirit for an artist. I have come to think that in art you have a relationship to the dead, you are as outside of life as you are inside, and that your art expresses the timeless as well as what's happening in your own time. That creates a mood and a kind of coloring of emotions and character that is gray.

When we read good books or when we study the work of someone who's gone before us, we're not just learning ideas or gathering information; we're establishing a connection to the dead. And that's a kind of gray thing to do. It doesn't have to be depressive exactly, but it is in that general area of this relationship to the dead. I feel that I have had a strong relationship to those who have gone before me, and when I write about them, I'm not just quoting their ideas because they're great ideas, but I'm actually feeling myself in dialogue and in relationship with them.

TS   You mentioned that during depression we can have experiences or insights that are not available during other states of being. Can you say more about that?

TM   When I said that, I was quoting James Hillman, who used to say that depression allows us an entry into imagination that no other mood can give us. In this way it is essential. When you are depressed, you may have certain thoughts, you may see the world in a certain way—as I did seeing it through aging—that you couldn't have seen any other way. To see getting older through a very happy spirit is probably different from seeing it with that sense of loss, of time wasted or opportunities missed. All of those things scoop you out and make you a deeper person. They may be painful experiences and they don't seem to be aimed at your personal growth, but nevertheless, they do something that's valuable for you; they make you a deeper, more thoughtful, and more reflective person. And that allows you to be closer to other people, because you don't approach them just from this happiness place, but with a certain level of seriousness. And you're not just a one-dimensional person—you have all these dimensions, including one that is rather depressive.

TS   I think it is very helpful to describe depression as a special doorway to the imagination, as so many take the experience of depression as evidence of a mistake or fundamental flaw that must be fixed or corrected.

TM   I agree that it's an important and very real thing, to have all these experiences that take us deep into dark places. If you lose something like a job, or go through a divorce and separate from a partner, or you get sick, these experiences can actually make you a deeper person. When it comes time for you to age and relate to the world in this older way, with wisdom and with something to offer the world—especially to younger people—those depressions are very useful because they've made you into someone who can think things through. Someone who has *lived* life. There is a feeling you get when you meet somebody who's getting a little older and resisting it and it seems they haven't really lived. That's a sad situation, because their youthfulness doesn't feel real.

I've had the opportunity in my life to be affected by two very important elderly people, including my father, who died at one hundred years of age. We became closest in the last decade of his life. He was a terrific influence on me, and he had a wonderful combination of a little depression and also great, good humor. When he got older, this fit him so well. I've never known anyone who had such a good mixture of youth and age at the same time. The second man, who turned one hundred years old recently, is a psychiatrist—a very accomplished and well-known man, who is also very sweet and thoughtful. He has been tormented by a certain kind of depression throughout his life, by things that happened in his youth. Despite that, he is a man of great joy and just a remarkable person.

I've known these two people in my life who have given me so much, they've lived so long, and they've kept their good humor and joy of life—despite a great deal of depression. In this way, they've brought depression into their old age in a way that has made them real and genuine, while still maintaining their youth. That youthfulness is also real and genuine. They're not trying to be young or denying their aging; they are really living out their youth.

There's a paradox at work here. If you can invite your depression in, you have a better chance that, as you get older, you will keep your youthfulness. This really is the secret of getting old. When we stop defending against age, or stop defending against being depressed, then life has a chance to come in. When you're defending against them and trying to get rid of them, there's no room for the vitality that you could have otherwise.

19

Depression as a Wake-Up Call

Jeff Foster

There's such a bias toward what we call the "positive" in our culture. We're supposed to be happy and attractive and successful. We're supposed to have the answers, to be able to hold it all together, to be in control, to be "up" all the time. Yet the truth is, sometimes we feel "down," and heartbroken, and lost, and devoid of answers. Sometimes it feels like everything is falling apart. Sometimes very natural energies—like sadness, anger, frustration, shame and guilt, even feelings of hopelessness and despair, even profound longings for home—just want to move in us, express in us, have their being in us. But we don't allow them.

I want to share with you how I came to see my depression as a giant wake-up call, an intelligent (and much misunderstood) invitation to shed the burden of "self," release identification with the past and future, and reconnect with the healing energy of the present moment, my true home.

I don't think I actually realized I was depressed until quite a bit into my twenties. I guess I had been depressed my whole life up until that point; I'd just never labeled it as *depression*. I actually thought the way I experienced reality was "normal." It sounds bizarre now, but I saw it as "normal" to feel down all the time, shut off from life, living in resistance. I felt as though life was this awful punishment from God, or some kind of impossible task that I was forever failing at. I felt like I was walking someone else's path, with no ideas of my own. I assumed that's how most people felt: lost and isolated. I don't think anyone around me knew how depressed I was. How would they? I kept everything in. I was so shy and withdrawn, so shut off from the world. I would often mask my terrible loneliness with humor or distract myself with food or television or computer games. My life was devoid of intimacy. Mornings were the worst. I remember never wanting to get out of bed. It was that feeling of not really wanting to be part of the world, not wanting to be a "person," not wanting to play the game of normality but not having the courage to step out of it either. I existed in this horrible realm, this void between living and dying, too scared to die but too scared to live, forever afraid to step into the Unknown.

BREAKDOWN AND BREAKTHROUGH

In my early twenties, I was working night shifts at the BBC Television Centre in London, fixing computers in the basement. Not quite the life that I'd hoped for. I had always wanted to be a filmmaker, wanted to tell stories and move people to tears, but I had been too lacking in self-confidence to pursue that path. I'd graduated in astrophysics from Cambridge University and had taken this technical job at the BBC hoping that somehow, perhaps, maybe, I would be able to migrate into some kind of creative role there. To be honest, I didn't really know what I was doing! I was so lost, wandering in the wilderness of modern Western life. I didn't know what I wanted, who I was, where I belonged, where I was heading. I felt overwhelmed, and so disconnected, from others, from my body, from my job, so confused. Where was my true home? Where were my people? Where was . . . life? I felt like I was always screaming on the inside. I was in a very intense relationship with a girl at the time. It was my first proper relationship, and I thought I'd found my savior in her. We were going to get married, have kids, everything. She was going to complete me, or so I hoped. I was grasping for love outside of myself, but I couldn't see it at the time. Then she broke up with me, and oh, the unbearable pain of losing my savior! I hated my life, my body, my job, my broken heart. I wanted to die.

Then one evening, I was brushing my teeth in my bathroom. I suddenly felt ill, feverish, began to vomit, and dropped to the floor. I woke up some time later in a pool of my own blood. I tried to scream for help, but no noise would come out. And I remember thinking, *"Okay. This is it, Jeff. This is the end."* I felt death breathing down my neck. And I think something hit me that evening, something that would begin to turn my life around. It's hard to put into words. But I think it was something to do with how the constant possibility of unexpected death made life—every moment of it—precious and infinitely meaningful.

Actually I wasn't "dying" at all. It turns out in the end that I just had glandular fever and I had swallowed too many painkillers on an empty stomach, and my body in its intelligence was ridding itself of all the toxins. But I hadn't known, and death had seemed real for the first time in my life. Lying in my hospital bed, I started asking myself questions. Questions like, "Who am I?" and "What is the purpose of my life?" and "What is death?" and "What cannot be doubted, even as everything else crumbles to dust?"—questions I'd never asked before. I had been educated at Cambridge University; I was intellectually very strong. I had a lot of knowledge inside me—facts, opinions, theories, beliefs. I could do very complex calculations about the rotation of planets, but I had never asked these primal questions with any great sincerity. But now, these questions were alive in me, burning. I needed real answers, not regurgitated ones. Life had brought me to my knees, in order to shock me into asking the most profound questions.

In the following weeks, as I recovered, I started devouring spiritual books. I read about the Buddha, about enlightenment, about who we truly are beyond our image of ourselves, and something deep and ancient yet timeless began to awaken in me. Up until that point, I had been a total atheist, a nonbeliever, whatever you want to call it. Up until that point, I'd had zero interest in anything remotely spiritual, religious, anything that couldn't be proved through science. But I think something had changed that night, something had started to crack open within me. I became fascinated with life once again, an innocent child, curious about the mystery of existence, curious about why we are alive at all. And so began a spiritual journey of deep self-inquiry, of turning toward life and beginning to embrace my deepest pain and longings, which eventually led to me becoming an author and teacher, meeting other brothers and sisters in the darkness, reminding them of their inner light.

ALLOWING ALL OF LIFE'S ENERGIES

Like many people on this planet, for most of my life I was just *not there*, not showing up for life. I was lost in the past and future, in "rewind" and "fast-forward," as I call it now. I was busy regretting what had happened in the past, rewinding, wishing my history had been different, mourning the loss of the "good days," longing for yesterday's joys. Or I was off in the near or distant future, fast-forwarding, craving a better day or fearing imagined circumstances or events. And so I was never really present, never really connected to the moment, to the Source. My breakdown had been life in its infinite intelligence saying, *"Jeff, be here now, because this moment is all there is, and it's a miracle."* I think that's what healing is really all about: learning to be present, learning to show up for the joy as well as the heartache of your life, the joy as well as the sorrow.

There's such a bias toward what we call the "positive" in our culture. We're supposed to be happy and attractive and successful. We're supposed to have the answers, to be able to hold it all together, to be in control, to be "up" all the time. Yet the truth is, sometimes we feel "down" and heartbroken and lost and devoid of answers. Sometimes it feels like everything is falling apart. Sometimes very natural energies like sadness, anger, frustration, shame and guilt, even feelings of hopelessness and despair, even profound longings for home just want to move in us, express in us, have their being in us! But we don't allow them. We've forgotten how to trust all of life's energies. We've been taught to label these parts of us as "dark," "sinful," "evil," or "negative," and push them away, destroy them, or distract ourselves from them. But these are just neglected parts of us that long for kind attention! They are not enemies at all. They long to be allowed into the light, without shame. There is such a richness of experience in us that is never honored, that gets pushed away into the darkness.

What I see now is that all feelings have a place in us, all feelings want to move in us, the joy as much as the sadness, the excitement as much as the fear, the certainty as much as the doubt. Even moments of despair and heartbreak have a place in our lives. And sometimes we *need* to touch the depths of our sadness, sometimes we *need* to feel the rawness of anger, sometimes we *need* to feel the vibration of loneliness in the belly. Just because we feel these things doesn't mean there's something wrong with us; it doesn't mean that we're sick or broken or far from awakening. It means that we are huge, we are vast, and all energies want to move in us! It means that these energies desperately want to be felt! It means all these energies are like our children, and they are all coming home to us! I truly believe that depression is the invitation to end the war with these neglected children of consciousness, to let go of resistance, welcome in all thoughts and feelings, and sink into deep rest in the present moment. From *de-pressed* to *deep rest*. That's the courageous journey that we are called to walk, whether we have been diagnosed with depression or not. The pathless journey toward loving the place where we stand.

BEGIN WHERE YOU ARE, WITH WHAT YOU HAVE

Your present experience is never a mistake! If, right now, you're feeling pain or grief or sadness or fear, or frustration is moving in you, or you don't know where to turn, or maybe you've experienced a loss and your heart is broken and raw, or maybe you're feeling a kind of sinking feeling in your belly, and you can't even work out why it's there . . . well, that's your experience right now! And we have to begin by acknowledging where we are, validating and honoring the place where we stand, for we may just be standing on sacred ground, even in our pain. We have to stop comparing ourselves to anything or anyone else! If change is going to come, it will come from a place where we are deeply accepting of this moment exactly as it is.

I would say this to you: Friend, I know this moment doesn't feel okay. I know your heart is broken, I know that the future seems unclear to you, I know you feel the absence of answers right now, I know you feel a terrible longing for something you cannot name, but I am here with you. Let's begin where we are. Let's not focus on the thousands of steps that will come on the path, but the place where we stand on the path right now. And there is only now! Know that many others have gone through what you are going through. Know that sometimes it seems darkest before the dawn. But instead of longing for the dawn and rejecting the darkness, let us touch the dark parts with gentleness and light. Let us meet what is here, not rush toward what is not yet here. For even the darkest cave may contain treasure, and even the most intense and uncomfortable feelings may actually contain strange medicine. Walk your path courageously, friend, and know that your loved ones walk with you.

Of course, it's natural to want to feel better right now, for things to be different from how they are. You don't want to feel this sadness; you want to feel joy. You don't want to feel this sinking in the stomach; you want to feel excitement and wonder and lightness, as you did when you were young and things seemed simpler. You don't want doubt; you want certainty. You don't want questions; you want answers. And so the mind says, "Well why isn't *that* here—why isn't the joy here? Why isn't the bliss here? Where did it go? When will answers come? What have I done wrong?" But wait a moment. It's totally understandable that you don't want to feel the way you feel now. But so quickly, in our longing for a brighter tomorrow, in our chasing of the "next" experience, we begin to reject or resist our present experience, today. But there is *only* today. Today is sacred. So today is where we must begin, if we are to begin. True healing begins when we stop seeking our rest and our joy in the past and future, when we stop disconnecting from where we are, and we become curious about this moment, reconnecting at the place where we stand.

A great way to begin to connect is through the body. The body is so deeply rooted in the present. Breathing happens in the present moment. Every breath is now. You do not breathe in the past or future; you breathe now. So become curious. Become fascinated. Allow your present experience to be the most fascinating thing in all of the universe. Bring gentle attention back to the breath. What is a breath? What's it like when air moves through the nostrils? Feel the expansion and contraction of the chest. Feel the belly rise and fall. Feel the life force move through you. Feel the vibrant life in each breath, feel where the air reaches in your body.

Feel the dance of sensations that we call the "body" happening now. Feel the aliveness of it. If you're feeling sorrow right now, if you're feeling fear, if you're feeling anger, well, where do you feel it in your body? I love that question. Come closer to yourself. Where do you feel the sorrow in the body? Where do you feel the loneliness in the body? That awful longing for something you cannot name, where does it hit you? Come closer. In your belly? Your chest? Your throat? Come back to present sensations. The raw sensations of life. Feel them without judging them, without pushing them away, without trying to make them disappear.

Healing can only happen in the present moment. We come out of the past and future, out of the big, epic story of "me and my depression," "me and my difficult life," and we touch what's actually here, beyond history and imagination, beyond dreams and plans. We're reconnecting with the tension in the stomach, or the empty feeling in the chest. Maybe these are not enemies or mistakes or blocks to awakening, but intelligent parts of ourselves that just want some loving attention. So instead of going into the mind, and trying to solve our depression, fix it, or find answers, let's reconnect with what's actually here in the moment. And let's ask, "Is there anything in this present moment, is there anything that wants some loving attention from me right now? Is there a tender place in me? A lost and lonely part that needs my warmth? Is there a fragile, vulnerable fragment here? Is there an unloved place that longs for some gentleness?" We're honoring some ancient commitment to stop abandoning our embodied human experience. We're actually using our depression constructively: it has asked us to slow down and come back to ourselves.

YOUR THOUGHTS ARE YOUR CHILDREN

For most of my life, I saw my mind as a torture chamber. I just never knew how to switch it off! So I was at war with all the energies in my body, *and* also at war with my thoughts. And the more I tried to ignore, repress, or numb myself to my thoughts, the louder they would become. What you resist persists—this seems to be a universal law.

"You're ugly and no one likes you. You're a failure. You're a waste of space. You're nothing!" I believed these thoughts, thought that they defined me. I would try to ignore them, or silence them by distracting myself, with television, with computer games, with food, and that's what led to me becoming a computer and food addict. It was all an attempt to run away from myself.

In reality, thoughts are just like bodily sensations—they are only parts of you (for there is only you) that want to belong. What thoughts are really saying is, "Excuse me! Hello! Can I be here? Is there enough room in you for me? Are you vast and spacious enough to allow me?" That's the kind of relationship I began to cultivate with thoughts—seeing them as my beloved children, not enemies. It's like I am a giant living movie screen, and all kinds of movies—comedies, tragedies, horror movies, war movies, romances—can appear and disappear in my embrace. All kinds of thoughts, pictures, and images can come and go in what I am. That's what the spiritual teachers mean when they talk about awareness. Awareness is this living movie screen, and thoughts are welcome to come and go on the screen. As the screen, no thought can define you or limit you or capture you. You are bigger than thoughts. You are not trapped in thoughts, but the space for thoughts. Thoughts don't need to "stop"; they need to be embraced.

There is a great power in noticing thoughts, observing their dance, instead of getting caught up in them. At any moment, we can silently observe thought activity. And that observation itself does not require thinking. It's not thought that sees thought—it's something beyond thought: awareness. This is one of the realizations that really began to change my life: *If I'm noticing thoughts, then those thoughts can't be who I truly am.* So just beginning to see yourself as the space *for* thoughts, however loud thoughts are, however intense thoughts are, however strange thoughts are, that's where the healing begins. You may even start saying to yourself, *"Okay, those are thoughts, just thoughts. I'm noticing thoughts, so the thoughts cannot be who I really am."* And then you get that sense that thoughts are coming and going *in* you, like waves arising and disappearing in the ocean, like clouds in the sky. You start to get the sense of yourself as something bigger than thoughts, something more spacious than thoughts. You come to know yourself as the vast ocean or the sky of awareness in which all thoughts come and go. And sometimes there are lots of clouds and sometimes there are very few clouds, but the effortless sky of You always remains. You are the space for the positive *and* the negative clouds, the light thoughts and the dark thoughts, the happy images and the sad images, thoughts that say, "I'm a success" and thoughts that say, "I'm a failure." You are the nondual awareness in which the play of duality—good and bad, happy and sad, light and dark—dances. You are neither a success nor a failure, beautiful nor ugly, rich nor poor, enlightened nor unenlightened—you are life itself, wide open, spacious, indefinable, mysterious, and perfect as you are, even with all your seeming imperfections.

THE URGE TO DIE IS THE URGE TO LIVE

Many people see suicide as a "way out" of their pain. I understand. I used to think of suicide all the time. In the midst of my pain, suicide to me seemed like the ultimate relief, the logical answer to the misery of my life. I just wanted to end the struggle, to find relief, to be infinite again, to return to Source—and killing myself was such a temptation. But I realize now what I really wanted wasn't to kill myself at all. It was more like this: *I wanted to live, but I didn't know how.* I wanted rest, so deeply and profoundly, but I didn't know how to get there. Life and love just seemed so far away. How could I return to the wonder? I had tasted it as a child—the wonder of life—and I think we all did when we were very, very young. We all tasted life, the immediacy of life, the joy of just being alive, of greeting a new day with gratitude and excitement. Even the most depressed people on some level must still remember that, the joy of existence, even if it's buried very, very deep down. That potential is still there. And so maybe the urge to die is really the urge to get back to that, that innocence, that simplicity. I didn't really want to jump in front of a train, or jump off a cliff, or slash my wrists—it wasn't what my heart really, truly longed for, to stop the functioning of the body. It couldn't have been. What I really longed for was life, the taste of life—to live, really live, without the heaviness of history and future, without the burden of "myself."

And of course life wasn't ever "far away." It was pulsating through my body, it was there in every breath, every beat of the heart, every sensation, every feeling, every thought, in every moment! It was there with me as I lay in bed wanting to die; it was the feeling of my body on the bedsheets, it was the feeling of the pillow under my head, it was every in-breath and every out-breath, it was the sweet sound of the birds singing on the tree next to my window. It was there—life was always there! I just couldn't see it, because I was seeking it!

I longed to be unlimited and free, but the truth is, I had never been limited and bound in the first place! None of us are limited or bound, not even the most "depressed" people! What I was—what we all are in essence—was the space for the in-breath and the out-breath, the awareness of every thump of the heart, the space for the sunlight on my face, and the tweeting of the bird near my window. I was the space for *all* of that, and life was present, life was right there, always! Life was even there in that feeling of sadness in my stomach from which I'd been running! That was life as well, that was *also* a complete expression of life! Sadness had a right to be there. Life was there even in the very longing for an escape *from* life! That was the cosmic joke of it: what I was longing *for* was right there screaming at me, even in that desperate longing for life, which I had confused with the longing for death. Life was right there *burning, sizzling, fizzling* as the sadness; it was life expressing itself fully and completely. Like many people in the world today, I had become blind to grace because I believed or I had been taught that it was far away from me, that I didn't deserve it because I wasn't good or holy or healthy or beautiful or perfect enough. In a way, I think we're all taught this. This is part of our conditioning, that basically we're undeserving of all the riches of the universe. But no, you are life, the power of suns moves in you. And you don't have to understand, for even your non-understanding is perfect!

A RETURN TO SIMPLICITY

Looking back, there was intelligence in life bringing me to my knees. There was intelligence in life sticking me in bed, making me lose all my interest in going to work, allowing me to lose all my interest in seeing friends, allowing me to lose all hope for the future, to lose all external meaning, even to lose the interest in getting out of bed. It was almost like life was stripping away all illusions, all distractions, to make me stay close to myself, to make me remember what was left after everything external was stripped away, to remember my own presence, essential and free, a miracle, bursting with life. My own presence, so simple yet overlooked for a lifetime, had always been with me, closer even than breathing, more undoubtable than anything. My own simple presence was the gift, what I had always been searching for. *I am here. I exist. I Am. And that is the greatest miracle of all.* Sometimes that's where you have to begin, at the very beginning. You have to get back to the origin of life, the "I Am." Depression did that for me—it made me surrender and begin again. It was like a spiritual reboot.

Your own presence! You've always known it. It's been the most intimate thing. Everything else in your life has come and gone: friends and lovers, successes and failures, wealth and poverty, the accolades, the highs and the lows, the times of great pain and the times of great joy, states and experiences both sacred and profane, both exciting and boring, even the most ecstatic spiritual experiences have all come and gone. But what's always remained, what has never come and gone, the simplest thing, the most essential thing is you, your own presence. You, before your imagination of yourself.

We never really know what's going to happen next in the movie of our lives. We never know what's going to happen in the next scene, and we can't get back to a previous scene. There is only this scene—this present moment. That is our place of contact, however imperfect or messy it seems. And sometimes we just need to stop and remember where we are: "I'm here. I'm here. It's this scene, and I can't know what's coming next, but I'm here and I can hear my heart beating and I can notice the in-breath and notice the out-breath and I can feel some warmth in my chest and I can feel some tightness in my belly and there's a sense of heaviness in the shoulders and there's the sound of a little bird singing outside, and can I begin to see the life in all of this? Can I stop pushing all of this away? Can I stop making all of this wrong? Can I stop fast-forwarding to the next scene? Can I stop rewinding to a previous scene? Can I turn toward this sacred scene, where all of life is, where the source of true power and healing is, and where all the answers will eventually grow? Can I feel the perfection in this beautifully imperfect moment? Can it be *okay* for me to feel *not okay* right now? Can I even trust *that?* Can I feel the certainty of my own existence, even if everything else seems uncertain right now? Can I fall in love with *where I am?*"

Perhaps in our pain and our heartbreak, in our brokenness and our despair, we are never, ever less than whole, and the future is always wide open.

Resources for Suicidal Depression and Ways to Help Yourself and Others

Karla McLaren

Suicidal feelings can be very isolating, and the lifelines offered here exist to give people the support they need to make it through the despairing periods in their lives. If you or anyone you know is feeling suicidal, please know or let them know that support and help are available immediately. You're not alone.

If you are feeling suicidal in the United States, you can call the National Suicide Prevention Lifeline at 1-800-273-TALK (8255) or visit suicidepreventionlifeline.org for resources.

If you are anywhere in the world, the International Association for Suicide Prevention has a list of crisis centers and suicide prevention centers across the globe that you can access online by visiting iasp.info/resources/index.php.

The World Health Organization also has information on suicide in countries throughout the world, and numerous links to help you learn more on their website, who.int/mental_health/prevention/suicide/suicideprevent/en/.

Please reach out if you're in pain.

LOOKING AT SUICIDAL URGES EMPATHICALLY

Suicidal feelings have a range from soft to intense, but if you are feeling any level of suicidal urges right now, don't feel as if you have to wait until you're in the throes of torment to reach out for help.

If you can learn to catch your suicidal urges when they're in the soft stage, you can often stop yourself from falling into a pit of desperation and torment. A post on my website called "Working through Depression" may help you identify suicidal urges early in their life cycle so that you can address them and find healing. Visit karlamclaren.com/ working-through-depression.

In the territory of the suicidal urge, your capacity for emotional awareness and articulation can literally save your life. Here is some vocabulary that may help you catch your suicidal urges before they become very intense. This list is a part of my "Emotional Vocabulary List," which you can download for free at karlamclaren.com.

Soft Suicidal Urges

- Depressed
- Dispirited
- Constantly irritated, angry, or enraged
- Helpless
- Impulsive
- Withdrawn
- Apathetic
- Lethargic
- Disinterested
- Pessimistic
- Purposeless
- Discouraged
- Isolated
- World-weary
- Humorless
- Listless
- Melancholy
- Flat
- Indifferent
- Feeling worthless

Mood-State Suicidal Urges

- Desperate
- Hopeless

- Despairing
- Morbid
- Sullen
- Desolate
- Miserable
- Overwhelmed
- Pleasureless
- Joyless
- Fatalistic
- Empty
- Passionless
- Bereft
- Crushed
- Drained

Intense Suicidal Urges

- Agonized
- Tormented
- Self-destructive
- Tortured
- Anguished
- Bleak
- Numbed
- Doomed
- Death-seeking
- Reckless
- Devastated
- Nihilistic

IF YOU ARE A CONCERNED FRIEND

Please remember: when people are feeling suicidal, they're not having a simple happiness deficiency or exhibiting a character flaw. Something very serious is going on.

If you don't know what to do, you can call the National Suicide Prevention Lifeline's hotline as a concerned friend (1-800-273-TALK [8255]), and they'll help you understand what to do. Here are some ideas from the Lifeline website:

How To Be Helpful to Someone Who Is Threatening Suicide

- Be direct. Talk openly and matter-of-factly about suicide.
- Be willing to listen. Allow expressions of feelings. Accept the feelings.
- Be nonjudgmental.
- Don't debate whether suicide is right or wrong, or whether feelings are good or bad.
- Don't lecture on the value of life.
- Get involved. Become available. Show interest and support.
- Don't dare him or her to do it.
- Don't act shocked. This will put distance between you.
- Don't be sworn to secrecy. Seek support.
- Offer hope that alternatives are available but do not offer glib reassurance.
- Take action. Remove means, such as guns or stockpiled pills.
- Get help from persons or agencies specializing in crisis intervention and suicide prevention.

Thank you for helping when people are feeling suicidal. Thank you for your emotional fluency and your willingness to reach out when others are in need. You make a difference.

THE FIVE BIGGEST MYTHS ABOUT SUICIDE (OR: WHAT YOU DON'T KNOW CAN HURT *EVERYONE*)

This comes from another great resource, SAVE: Suicide Awareness Voices of Education, save.org.

1. **People who talk about suicide won't really do it.**

    Not True. Almost everyone who commits or attempts suicide has given some clue or warning. Do not ignore suicide threats. Statements like "You'll be sorry when I'm dead" and "I can't see any way out"—no matter how casually or jokingly said—may indicate serious suicidal feelings.

2. **Anyone who tries to kill him/herself must be crazy.**

    Not True. Most suicidal people are not psychotic or insane. They may be upset, grief stricken, depressed, or despairing, but extreme distress and emotional pain are often signs of mental illness and are not signs of psychosis.

3. **If a person is determined to kill him/herself, nothing is going to stop him/her.**

    Not True. Even the most severely depressed person has mixed feelings about death, and most waver until the very last moment between wanting to live and wanting to die. Most suicidal people do not want to die; they want the pain to stop. The impulse to end it all, however overpowering, does not last forever.

4. **People who commit suicide are people who were unwilling to seek help.**

    Not True. Studies of suicide victims have shown that more than half had sought medical help within six months of their death and a majority had seen a medical professional within one month of death.

5. Talking about suicide may give someone the idea.

    Not True. You don't give a suicidal person morbid ideas by talking about suicide. The opposite is true—bringing up the subject of suicide and discussing it openly is one of the most helpful things you can do.

TALK ABOUT SUICIDE AND LET PEOPLE KNOW YOU'LL LISTEN

Suicidal feelings can affect anyone, from kids to elders. Let your friends and family know that you're willing to talk about suicide; you may save someone's life, certainly, but you'll also make life easier and less awful for people who are suffering.

Thank you for making the world more empathic and compassionate.

May we all find peace and healing; may we all find ways to reduce suffering in the world.

Index

Note: Page numbers in italics indicate figures.

About the Contributors

Amy Weintraub, MFA, E-RYT 500, founding director of the Life-Force Yoga Healing Institute, author of *Yoga for Depression* and *Yoga Skills for Therapists: Effective Practices for Mood Management,* has been a pioneer in the field of yoga and mental health for more than twenty years. Amy's recovery from depression began more than thirty years ago on her meditation cushion, but it wasn't until she added the physical practice and breathing of yoga that her "empty pockets" began to overflow with gratitude. She is passionate about contributing to the growing body of research on the benefits of yoga for optimum mental health, and the LifeForce Yoga protocol has been the basis for a number of published papers. This evidence-based protocol is being used by health-care providers around the world and is featured in the LifeForce Yoga® CD Series, as well as in the first DVD home yoga practice series for mood management: the award-winning *LifeForce Yoga to Beat the Blues, Level 1 & Level 2.* Visit yogafordepression.com.

Ann Marie Chiasson, MD, MPH, is board certified in Family Medicine and in Hospice and Palliative Medicine. She completed a fellowship in Integrative Medicine and is a Clinical Assistant Professor of Medicine for Arizona Center for Integrative Medicine at the University of Arizona, where she teaches integrative medicine, energy healing, meditation, and ceremony. She also works as a hospice physician at Casa de la Luz Hospice in Tucson, Arizona, and has a private integrative and energy medicine practice in Tucson. She is the author of the book *Energy Healing: The Essentials of Self-Care* (Sounds True, 2013) as well as a DVD, *Energy Healing for Beginners* (Sounds True, 2011), and a home study course, *Energy Healing: The Essentials of Self-Care* (Sounds True, 2011). She is co-author of *Self-Healing with Energy Medicine* (Sounds True, 2009) with Dr. Andrew Weil. For more information, go to annmariechiassonmd.com.

Christina Baldwin is a writer, presenter, speaker, and storycatcher. She has written many books about the importance of life stories, the empowerment of journal writing, and, with her partner, Ann Linnea, created a modern methodology of circle practice that calls people and organizations into conversations of heart and purpose. Christina and Ann have recently taught circle across the United States and Canada, Europe, and Australia. Through Sounds True, she produced the audio set *Lifelines: How Personal Writing Can Save Your Life*. Her most recent books are *Storycatcher: Making Sense of our Lives through the Power and Practice of Story* and, with Ann Linnea, *The Circle Way: A Leader in Every Chair*. She looks forward to increasing time spent in the Pacific Northwest to take up the next phase of her writing and community life. Visit peerspirit.com for the breadth of her work.

Elizabeth Rabia Roberts, EdD, is a spiritual teacher, global educator, and international peace and justice activist. She has worked and lived in more than a dozen countries as diverse as Burma, Brazil, Syria, Iran, and Afghanistan. She has co-created four educational programs, including Naropa University's masters of arts degree in environmental leadership and eco-psychology certificate program. With her husband, she leads peace pilgrimages throughout the Middle East. Rabia is an initiated Shieka in the Sufi Way and also a teacher in the Buddhist nondual tradition. She has guided wilderness quests for more than twenty-five years, and mentors social-activist and quest guides. She is co-author of *Earth Prayers* and *Prayers for a Thousand Years,* and received her doctorate at Harvard University and her master's degree in liberation theology at Marquette University. Rabia Roberts has lived with depression for more than thirty-five years, and knows its depths and transformational powers. She frequently counsels people who struggle with this rite of passage. Visit wakinguptogether.org and pathofthefriend.org.

James S. Gordon, MD, is a world-renowned expert in using mind-body medicine to heal depression, anxiety, and psychological trauma, and is the founder and director of the Center for Mind-Body Medicine. Dr. Gordon is a clinical professor in the departments of Psychiatry and

Family Medicine at Georgetown Medical School, and he served as chairman of the White House Commission on Complementary and Alternative Medicine Policy. Visit cmbm.org.

Jeff Foster studied astrophysics at Cambridge University. In his mid-twenties, after a long period of depression and illness, he became addicted to the idea of spiritual enlightenment and embarked on an intensive quest for the ultimate truth of existence. His search came crashing down with the recognition of the nondual nature of everything and the discovery of the extraordinary in the ordinary. Life became what it always was: intimate, open, loving, and spontaneous, and Jeff was left with a deep understanding of the root illusion behind all human suffering as well as a love of the present moment. Jeff was voted number fifty-nine on Watkins Mind Body Spirit's 2014 list of the world's 100 Most Spiritually Influential Living People. He has published five books in more than seven languages, including *The Deepest Acceptance* and *Falling in Love with Where You Are*. He at present holds meetings, retreats, and private one-to-one sessions around the world. His website is lifewithoutacentre.com.

Jennifer L. Holder received her master's of publishing degree in 2003 and has worked in book publishing in Canada, England, and Manhattan. She has been an editor at Sounds True since 2011.

Karla McLaren, MEd, is an award-winning author, researcher, and pioneering educator whose empathic approach to emotions revalues even the most "negative" emotions and opens startling new pathways into the depths of the soul. As a lifelong hyper-empath, Karla has developed a grand unified theory of emotions that melds original theory with her work with survivors of dissociative trauma and extensive research into the social and biological sciences. Karla has also developed a unified Six Essential Aspects of Empathy model that explicitly and intentionally welcomes people who have been exiled from earlier models of empathy (such as men, boys, and autistic people). Karla is the author of *The Art of Empathy: A Complete Guide to Life's Most Essential Skill,*

The Language of Emotions: What Your Feelings Are Trying to Tell You, and the multimedia online course *Emotional Flow: Becoming Fluent in the Language of Emotions.* Her website is karlamclaren.com.

Mark Nepo is beloved as a poet, teacher, and storyteller, and has been called "one of the finest spiritual guides of our time," "a consummate storyteller," and "an eloquent spiritual teacher." He has published fifteen books and recorded nine audio projects, including his number-one *New York Times* bestseller *The Book of Awakening.* His work has been translated into more than twenty languages. Recent work includes *The Endless Practice* and *Reduced to Joy* (in both book and audio-teaching formats). Mark has appeared several times with Oprah Winfrey on her *Super Soul Sunday* program on OWN TV, and has also been interviewed by Robin Roberts on *Good Morning America.* About this anthology, Mark says, "There is no bypassing the human journey. Only when we can engage in an honest and open conversation like this does the magnificent resilience of the human spirit reveal itself." Please visit Mark at marknepo. com, threeintentions.com, and info@wmespeakers.com.

Mary Pipher, PhD, graduated from UC Berkeley in 1969 with a degree in cultural anthropology. Later, she received her PhD in clinical psychology from the University of Nebraska at Lincoln. She worked as a therapist, which offered a wonderful vantage point on the human race. In her forties, she began her writing career. *Reviving Ophelia* was her first book. Since then she has written about families, the elderly, refugees, advocacy, and her own life. Her most recent book, *The Green Boat,* tackles our denial and sense of helplessness in the face of global climate change to chart a path toward hope and action. Regardless of her topics, Mary has written with the goal of increasing intentionality, moral imagination, and kind behavior in her readers. She has lived a lucky life, but also a hard life, and takes great comfort in the natural world, in activism, in writing, and in her community of friends and family.

Michael Bernard Beckwith is the founder of Agape International Spiritual Center, a multicultural, transdenominational community with thousands of local members and live streamers throughout the world. Beckwith's humanitarian works have been read into the 107th *Congressional Record,* and in 2012 he addressed the UN General Assembly during its annual World Interfaith Harmony Conference. Beckwith is co-chair of the Gandhi King Season for Nonviolence, which was launched at the United Nations in 1998, and is active in 900 international cities and 67 countries. He is the author of *Life Visioning, Spiritual Liberation,* and *TranscenDance.* He has appeared on *Dr. Oz, Larry King Live,* the *Oprah Winfrey Show, Tavis Smiley,* and in his own PBS Special, *The Answer Is You.* Every Friday at 1 p.m. PST, thousands tune in to his radio show on KPFK, *Wake Up: The Sound of Transformation.* For more information, visit agapelive.com.

Parker J. Palmer, PhD, is founder and senior partner of the Center for Courage & Renewal. A writer, speaker, and activist who received his PhD in sociology from the University of California at Berkeley, Palmer has had his work recognized with eleven honorary doctorates. His nine books—which include *Let Your Life Speak, The Courage to Teach,* and *Healing the Heart of Democracy*—have sold more than a million copies. In 1998, the Leadership Project, a national survey of 10,000 educators, named him one of the thirty "most influential senior leaders" in higher education. In 2010, he received the William Rainey Harper Award, whose previous recipients include Margaret Mead, Elie Wiesel, and Paolo Freire. In 2011, the *Utne Reader* named him one of twenty-five visionaries on its annual list of "People Who are Changing the World." Recently, when he received a Distinguished Alumni Achievement Award and was asked to name his most important achievement, he responded, "Surviving three bouts with clinical depression." This was printed in the program, but no one in the audience of hundreds said anything about it.

Reginald A. Ray, PhD, draws on four decades of study and practice within the Tibetan Buddhist tradition to address the unique spiritual imperatives of modern people. He is the founder and spiritual director of the Dharma Ocean Foundation, a nonprofit educational organization dedicated to the practice, study, and preservation of the teachings of Chögyam Trungpa Rinpoche and the practice lineage he embodied. The first full-time faculty member and chair of the Buddhist Studies (later Religious Studies) Department at Naropa University, he is the author of *Touching Enlightenment, Indestructible Truth, Secret of the Vajra World,* and other books, and has recorded several Sounds True audio programs, including *Your Breathing Body* and *Mahamudra for the Modern World.* Dr. Ray regularly leads meditation retreats at Blazing Mountain Retreat Center in Crestone, Colorado. For more information and access to free recordings of dharma talks and guided meditations, please visit dharmaocean.org.

Robert Augustus Masters, PhD, is an author, relationship expert, and pioneering psychotherapist with a doctorate in psychology. He's the cofounder, with his wife, Diane, of the Masters Center for Transformation, a school featuring relationally rooted psycho-spiritual work devoted to deep healing and fully embodied awakening. His books include *Transformation Through Intimacy, Spiritual Bypassing, Emotional Intimacy,* and *To Be a Man.* His uniquely integral and uncommonly deep work, developed over the past thirty-seven years, intuitively blends the psychological and physical with the spiritual, emphasizing full-blooded embodiment, authenticity, emotional openness and literacy, deep shadow work, and the development of relational maturity. At essence, his work is about becoming more intimate with *all* that we are—high and low, dark and light, ephemeral and enduring—in the service of the deepest possible healing, awakening, and integration. He works side by side and in very close conjunction with Diane. His website is robertmasters.com.

Sally Kempton is a respected teacher of applied spiritual wisdom, known for her capacity to kindle meditative states in others, and to help students work with meditative experience as a framework for practical life-change. She has spent over four decades delving deeply into meditation and self-inquiry, practicing and teaching the nondual tantric models for working with emotional states. Sally teaches teleclasses, retreats, and workshops, and is on the faculty at Esalen and Kripalu. She is the author of the best-selling book *Awakening Shakti: The Transformative Power of the Goddesses of Yoga* and of *Meditation for the Love of It,* which *Spirituality and Health* magazine called "the meditation book your heart wants you to read." Her audio program, *Doorways to the Infinite: The Art and Practice of Tantric Meditation,* was released by Sounds True in 2014. A former swami in a Vedic tradition, Sally's work is grounded in the nondual tantric tradition of Kashmir Shaivism. She is versed in the theory and practice of yoga and tantra, along with an ability to integrate yogic wisdom with contemporary psychology and integral thought. Her website is sallykempton.com, and her books and CDs are available through SoundsTrue.com.

Sandra Ingerman, is the author of ten books, including *Soul Retrieval* and *Walking in Light,* the presenter of seven audio programs, and the creator of the Transmutation App. Sandra is an internationally renowned teacher on shamanism and shamanic healing. She is also a licensed Marriage and Family therapist, Professional Mental Health Counselor, and board-certified expert on traumatic stress. Sandra is passionate about teaching shamanic journeying and healing, how to use spiritual practices as a global community for planetary healing, and is devoted to teaching people how to reconnect with nature. Her parents, Aaron and Lee Ingerman, were role models for how to forge ahead despite life's challenges. Engaging in daily shamanic practices provides the tools she needs to feel empowered and passionate about life. To read articles written by Sandra, listen to interviews, and read her monthly column, "Transmutation News," visit sandraingerman.com. To find a local shamanic practitioner or teacher, visit shamanicteachers.com.

Susan Piver is a Buddhist teacher and the *New York Times* best-selling author of eight books, including the award-winning *How Not to Be Afraid of Your Own Life* and her latest, *The Wisdom of a Broken Heart,* which explores the dark power of sadness more fully. Her next book, *Start Here Now: A Guide to the Path and Practice of Meditation,* will be published next year. She teaches workshops and speaks all over the world. She is a student of Sakyong Mipham Rinpoche and has been practicing in the Shambhala Buddhist lineage since 1995. In 2012, Piver created the Open Heart Project to deliver meditation instruction and support to anyone who might want it, via two guided meditations per week accompanied by a short talk or insight into the practice. There are currently close to 12,000 members all over the world, making this an early example of a completely virtual sangha. Visit susanpiver.com.

Thomas Moore, PhD, published *Care of the Soul,* a classic bestseller, in 1992. His most recent book, *A Religion of One's Own,* is his twentieth published book. He has been a psychotherapist for almost forty years and often teaches spiritual leaders and psychiatrists, and at Jung societies and medical organizations. In his youth, he was a Catholic monk for thirteen years, and he draws on that experience in all his writing. Thomas also has a background in music composition and writes fiction. He is married to Hari Kirin Khalsa, a leader in Kundalini yoga and an accomplished painter. His daughter, Ajeet, is a rising star in spiritual music, and his stepson, Abe, is doing graduate studies in architectural design. Thomas always works at blending soul and spirit, sacred and secular, art and life, ideas and living.

Traleg Kyabgon Rinpoche IX (1955–2012) was devoted to bringing Buddhism in its purist form to the West. In addition to undergoing the rigorous and traditional education of a *tulku* from the Tibetan Buddhist tradition, Rinpoche studied Western philosophy, psychology, and comparative religion. His excellent command of English ensured that Rinpoche imparted the essence of the Buddhist teachings in the most profound and practical way. He gave both a thorough intellectual explanation of how the mind works and the tools to better manage the mind. In teachings and books, Rinpoche offers meditational practices and contemplations to help overcome debilitating mental states that can become habitually embedded. In his teachings on managing depression, emotions, and similar topics, Rinpoche explains how we can create a more positive mental environment conducive to dissolving negativity more easily rather than allowing negativity to reside and dominate the mind. Rinpoche developed a network of centers, including the E-Vam Institute and Nyima Centre in Australia, New Zealand, and New York. He taught extensively through Europe and Southeast Asia, and his publications include *The Essence of Buddhism, Mind at Ease, The Practice of Lojong,* and *The Four Dharmas of Gampopa.* For more information, visit tralegrinpoche.org.

About Sounds True

Sounds True is a multimedia publisher whose mission is to inspire and support personal transformation and spiritual awakening. Founded in 1985 and located in Boulder, Colorado, we work with many of the leading spiritual teachers, thinkers, healers, and visionary artists of our time. We strive with every title to preserve the essential "living wisdom" of the author or artist. It is our goal to create products that not only provide information to a reader or listener, but that also embody the quality of a wisdom transmission.

For those seeking genuine transformation, Sounds True is your trusted partner. At SoundsTrue.com you will find a wealth of free resources to support your journey, including exclusive weekly audio interviews, free downloads, interactive learning tools, and other special savings on all our titles.

To learn more, please visit SoundsTrue.com/freegifts or call us toll-free at 800-333-9185.